elemental knits

a *perennial* knitwear collection

COURTNEY
spainhower

 Interweave

Dedication

*For my girls, as always. My light, my life.
In loving memory of my grandmother, my
biggest fan: Jeanette Russo, 1931–2018.*

EDITORIAL DIRECTOR Kerry Bogert

EDITOR Nathalie Mornu

EDITORIAL COORDINATOR Hayley DeBerard

TECHNICAL EDITOR Kristen TenDyke

ART DIRECTOR & DESIGNER Ashlee Wadeson

INTERIOR LAYOUT pnormandesigns

ILLUSTRATORS Ann Swanson & Kristen TenDyke

PHOTOGRAPHER Harper Point Photography

STYLIST Tina Gill

HAIR/MAKEUP Jessica Johnston & Valerie Salls

Interweave

penguinrandomhouse.com

13 5 7 9 10 8 6 4 2

ISBN-13: 978-1-63250-653-5

Contents

Introduction

Welcome to *Elemental Knits*.

This book is for those who aspire to be less wasteful, more comfortable, and ever stylish. It achieves this by providing knitting patterns that enhance a capsule wardrobe, arranged by season. This type of wardrobe asks us to look within, be honest with ourselves about our needs, embrace less excess, and craft an outward appearance that truly reflects our inner spirit. Crafting a capsule wardrobe is an ongoing trend that speaks more about the *minds* of women today than about their closets.

Conceived in the 1970s by Susie Faux, a boutique owner in London, the capsule wardrobe is a set of versatile basics that won't go out of style, work well together to fashion many different outfits, and can be organized by season. A capsule wardrobe likely includes timeless blouses, pants, skirts, and coats that wouldn't be considered trendy; think straight slacks and buttoned blouses in a neutral palette. The capsule wardrobe was brought into the mainstream in America by Donna Karan in the 1980s. Since then, the concept has been gaining momentum, with many people embracing the concept of "less is more" and shifting from a wholly consumerist approach of owning many poorly made garments to possessing fewer garments but of superior quality.

Slow fashion is gaining impetus for good reason. There's a shift in our thinking about what's important in fashion and how we can adjust our day-to-day lives to honor those sensibilities. As you make your way through this book, you'll find haikus inspired by the four seasons. Japanese culture has, over time, cultivated a love for expression that follows a path of least resistance—a deceptively simple way to communicate through a few words of prose or a few strokes of ink. The haikus found within these pages are a tribute to the art of pruning back large, complicated ideas to their core, and they're where I drew a lot of inspiration

for this collection. I've designed versatile cardigans, timeless pullovers, and handsome accessories that supplement a capsule with their simplicity and versatility, and with details that ensure you won't find anything like them on racks in stores. These pieces won't be forgotten about in your closet.

In addition to focusing on patterns designed for daily wear within a curated, pared-down wardrobe, the core focus of this book is seasonal garments made with seasonally appropriate fibers. As knitters, we're not simply garment technicians; we're textile creators, and our textiles should be suitable for the season they're meant to be worn in. Beyond appropriate fibers, I've carefully selected yarns from people and companies that are in tune with the state of our world today and who go to great lengths to produce materials that are ethical and sustainable. Though it wasn't easy to source all plant-dyed and organic fibers for a collection of this size—twenty projects—and within the color palette I created for each chapter, I chose each yarn with those criteria in mind. Some yarns are produced by independent dyers, some are from companies that provide living wages to women in developing areas, and many are from businesses that use sustainable and organic farming practices or recycled materials. After some of the patterns, you'll find a company spotlight in which I share information about the yarn company, its founder, and their mission. The spotlights also dive deeper into my reasoning for choosing each of the yarns and why I feel the companies deserved a place on the stage.

I'm grateful to have you on this journey into the slow capsule wardrobe with me, sharing the new breed of thinking it represents. May you enjoy these knitted pieces for seasons to come.

chapter one

Beyond the Basics

When you begin to dive deeper and with intention into the construction of garments that have purpose—ones that are practical and get the most wear each season, and that you'll reach for year after year no matter the trends—it requires getting down to the details of pattern features and fiber content.

The collection in this book provides multiple patterns for each season, and the recommended yarns for each one take the guesswork out of fiber content for you. The garments for the transitional seasons of spring and autumn contain blended yarns that include sustainable superwash wool and silk so that they breathe but are also warm against cool air. Plant fibers dominate summer items for good reason: cotton, linen, and plant fiber blends in fine-weight yarns stay cool and are ideal for wearing against the skin. The winter garments, not surprisingly, are packed with wool or wool blended with warming fibers like alpaca. These are worked in heavier-weight yarns or in colorwork as an added shield against the cold.

Each piece is designed with specific pattern features in mind that encourage a certain fit, such as stretchy shoulder seams or clean, reinforced hems. But the collection also offers patterns that range from unfussy pieces with simple lines for easy styling to garments made for layering, constructed with unfastened fronts or ample ease for wear with tees, thermals, or button-up blouses. Many of the pieces will appeal to those of you who love adding color and texture to their basic capsule wardrobe.

PALETTES & INSPIRATIONS

Over the next few pages, you'll see the sketches I originally drew of the patterns I wanted to make for this book. As I knitted up the samples, they sometimes changed in small ways, but the silhouettes remain unmistakable. Before I designed, I made lists of the words that each season evokes for me. These pages also include photos of the fibers I selected, and some of the swatches I knitted up to test whether the yarn would work in the stitch I planned to feature. I gave each chapter its own palette, as every season speaks a different language, emits its own odor, and sings its own song.

Spring

- new growth
- frosty mornings
- chilled noses with flushed cheeks
- peach and pink buds
- muddy and wet
- chilly and sunny
- frosty and green

Akira

Samba

Gen

Clara

Hanne

Idalia

Solange

Dax

Nikko

Isla

Summer

- hot and sticky, but becoming dry
- once-green grass and gardens begin to pale
- glowing, sun-kissed shoulders
- sand and stone
- muted green of dry grasses
- warm and dry
- beaches and deserts under yellow skies

Autumn

- sunlight grows cooler
- nature's dying breath is exhaled in rich, jewel colors
- earthy and damp without being drab
- turning leaves
- crackling fires
- haunting sunsets
- indigo skies return

Hasan

Abi

Connac

Qui

Farah

Winter

- holiday cranberries and plum pie
- darkness
- cold and ice
- bare trees
- steamy breath
- conifers and snow drifts
- the musk of pine and cinnamon

Quilo

Demetria

Eira

Neve

Luni

knitting insights

Knitting has a language all its own; as knitters, pattern fluency takes us far. I don't design for the first-time knitter, but I do want to write patterns that can be knit by folks with a wide variety of skills and give new knitters the confidence to tackle something beyond scarves and hats. Below, you'll find a bit of information to help you understand patterns in general, along with more advanced tips that even someone with a lot of experience may not have come across before.

PATTERN-READING BASICS

There are clues tucked into each pattern that will help you create knitted garments that match the sample shown with confidence. The key is to know and understand these clues.

Understanding Sizing

Sizing is one of those questions that seems to arise time and time again. So how do you decide what size to make? Crafting a capsule is about finding the right fit for your style and taste, so start with your bust measurement. For this entire collection, the pattern sizes are listed by bust circumference. If you make the top in the size that matches your bust measurement, it will hang on your body as shown on the model in the photo.

> ### How to Measure Bust Size
>
> To measure your bust size, wrap a sewing tape measure around the fullest part of your bust, allowing the tape to be comfortably snug. This number is your actual bust measurement.

However, you have the option of deciding how much ease you want. When you deal with ease, you have an endless number of factors to consider, such as the shape of the garment, the intended fit, and how you plan to style it, to name a few. A more fitted design will have less ease and will measure closer to the actual bust of the wearer, while a garment with a relaxed or casual fit will have 4 inches (10 cm) or more of ease added to the bust measurement.

All of the patterns in this book list the ease I designed into the garment. If you want a closer fit than is shown in the photo, knit a smaller size; for a looser fit, make it in a larger size.

You may find that your bust size falls somewhere between the measurements listed. This is common; I almost always find myself between sizes, too! If this is the case, you can simply decide if you'd

like a garment that's slightly looser or snugger than shown in the photo. Something to also consider when making your decision is that neck openings, sleeve lengths, body lengths, and sleeve fit are all going to differ as well. I tend to prefer loose and casual and will choose a size slightly larger almost every time. However, if a sweater is shown far roomier than I would normally wear, I'll choose a size slightly smaller. This is personal preference, but if you're still uncertain, the measurements on the schematic can give you still more information to guide your decision. Take your hip and upper-arm measurements, compare them to the schematic, and think about how you'll wear the piece to help you decide which size to knit.

Knowing Your Right from Your Left

Many times, especially when reading a sweater pattern, you'll see sections that tell you to work, say, the "Right Front" or "Left Back." It's important to remember that these always refer to the wearer's right/left or front/back, rather than the garment in relation to you when knitting. The "right side" and "wrong side" refer to the side of the fabric that faces out when worn, with the right side being the "public" side of the garment.

Continuing to Work in Pattern

Here are some tips for when you come across the instructions "cont in est patt" while also needing to follow charts at the same time, as you will in the project called Cormac. When there are charts involved, I often use a pencil to mark where on the chart I'm at for each row while working easy-to-memorize patterns by reading the fabric. What does "reading the fabric" mean? Well, knitters who have a basic understanding of how knit and purl stitches look and who are able to determine the right side and the wrong side of the work are able to "read" the knitting. With more experience, knitters will learn to see what different increase and decrease stitches look like, too, and any errors will look like obvious marks in the fabric. This is a skill that comes with experience, but being patient, taking your time, and making notes as needed to keep track of where you've left off will make the task much easier and more enjoyable.

There are also times when you may have to increase or decrease in pattern. If there's a chart available for the stitches, make use of that trusty pencil again and mark where your increases or decreases are, so that it's easier to determine how you should proceed. For simple patterns such as ribbing, simply continue the pattern by reading your fabric, making notes as needed. Again, this can take a bit of practice, but once you begin to trust yourself to read your knitting, it will become second nature

SUBSTITUTING YARN

I created a color palette for each of the seasons and let that inspire my color selections for the garments I knit up for this book, but when you're selecting yarns for your own projects, keep your personal palette in mind. This may seem obvious, but I feel it's important to talk about in the realm of yarn substitutions.

I realize that many times suggested yarns are substituted with ones that are less expensive and, often, of lesser quality. Something I've said for years, and I believe will forever ring true, is that knitting provides a unique opportunity to create and re-create because of the nature of quality yarns. I find comfort in knowing I can unravel any garment or accessory that no longer has a home in my regular wear rotation and reuse the yarn to make something more current and useful. I can't uncut fabric, but I can always unknit yarn. This is a necessary feature for those on a budget who can't always afford miles and miles of high-quality materials. When you invest in a quality yarn that you can rip and repurpose, it not only furthers your ability to diminish waste, but stretches your dollars in the end, too. With that said, yarn substitution is inevitable at times because the recommended yarn may be discontinued or unavailable, and so I'm including information here on finding the best substitution for any given yarn.

With any project, there are three core aspects that should remain consistent when you select yarns other than the one recommended:

Yarn Weight

The yarn weight should always remain consistent when substituting, so that you can get the correct gauge and your garment fits as intended. When comparing yarn labels, make sure the gauge from the potential substitute is the same as the recommended yarn. This can be tricky because yarns are often listed in the pattern simply as "worsted" when the potential substitute may actually be a light worsted and the rec-ommended yarn may actually be a heavy worsted.

For example, the yarn recommended for Quilo is listed as worsted weight on the label, and the recommended gauge is 18–22 sts for 4" (10 cm) on size U.S. 6–8 needles. However, the yarn recom-mended for Neve is also listed as worsted weight on its label, and the recommended gauge is 17–21 sts for 4" (10 cm) on size U.S. 5–9 needles. These two yarns wouldn't be interchangeable.

I also don't recommend depending solely on the gauge listed on the pattern, either. When a pattern is written, it features gauge that is worked in a specific stitch like lace or cables, or on larger/smaller needles than recommended to obtain specific drape or structure in the fabric. I'll repeat this because it's important: To avoid a load of problems down the road, make sure the recommended gauge for the yarn listed matches the recommended gauge on the label of the yarn you plan to substitute.

Fiber Content

As knitters, our textiles should be appropriate for the season they're meant to be utilized in. The fibers that make up the yarn are significant not only because of the qualities they bring when worn—linen isn't suitable for a winter colorwork sweater, for example, because it's not warm and the fiber is too slippery to hold the colorwork and floats behind the fabric—but because different fibers behave differently when knit and washed. For example, alpaca is warm and might be tempting to substitute for wool, but it has a lot of drape and will become very loose over time, whereas wool is springy and holds its shape quite well. It's best to trust the designer when it comes to fiber content and use the same kind to ensure your project turns out as intended.

Yarn Ply

This is the least important consideration when choosing a substitution, but it's something to keep in mind. A project that has a lot of lace will likely have been designed using a single-ply or 2-ply yarn. Those yarns open nicely for lace and let the delicate eyelets breathe. Substitute a round, bouncy yarn, and it will fill in the holes in eyelets. So unless the garment uses minimal lace as an accent, that yarn likely isn't suitable. There are exceptions to every rule, but it's something to be mindful of and is often overlooked.

MAKING SWATCHES

For any garment, you need to knit a swatch. Making the swatch itself doesn't need to be a chore. Not only is a swatch about checking gauge, but swatching is also the perfect opportunity to get to know the yarn you'll be working with. You can learn a lot about a fiber—how stretchy and bouncy it is or how slack and silky it is, and if it "blooms" or develops a subtle haze while you work with it. If the yarn is a substitute for the suggested yarn in the given pattern, is it the best choice for substitution? A swatch can help you find out. A little swatch is also a great way to knit on the go. I find myself knitting swatches when I'm out and about and not in a position to be shackled to a pattern. For example, when I'm waiting on my kids in the car, waiting for an appointment, or meeting a friend for a drink after a long week, it's easier to whip up a square than it is to work complicated shaping or stitches in these situations.

There are a couple rules of thumb to follow when swatching for any garment:

Knitting Swatches Flat or Round

The pattern will state whether the gauge is obtained by working flat or in rounds, and this can be a very important detail for those whose knit rows and purl rows show greatly varied tension. If the gauge calls for rounds, you should knit a swatch in rounds by working on a 16-inch (40.5 cm) circular needle and sliding the work to the opposite end to begin another RS row after each row. This is simple, quick, and effective for swatching rounds.

Swatch Size

You'll want to knit a swatch large enough to measure out at least 2" (5 cm) of the pattern for gauge, if not more, but it doesn't always have to be a swatch 4 to 6 inches (10–15 cm) square. If the gauge listed is for Stockinette Stitch and you're a rather even knitter, knitting 3 × 3 inches (7.5 × 7.5 cm) should be plenty.

BLOCKING SWATCHES

Yep, that's right: Blocking is a must with swatches, too. There are a few key reasons for this. First, you want to get that gauge close so that your garment fits as intended. However, you also want to have an idea of how the yarn you're working with expands and settles after being washed or steamed. Getting an idea of this behavior is essential, since every yarn blocks differently due to its unique fiber blends, ply, twist, and weight. And lastly, any cables, colorwork, or lace will change drastically after blocking, so it's impossible to get gauge without this essential step.

If you find you're having trouble getting gauge for rows but not stitches, even after adjusting your needle size, try using needles made of a different material. This topic has been written about in depth, but many people are still unaware of these facts. Wooden needles tend to give the shortest row count and largest stitch count, followed by plastic, then metal. Super-slick metal needles yield the largest row count and smallest stitch count.

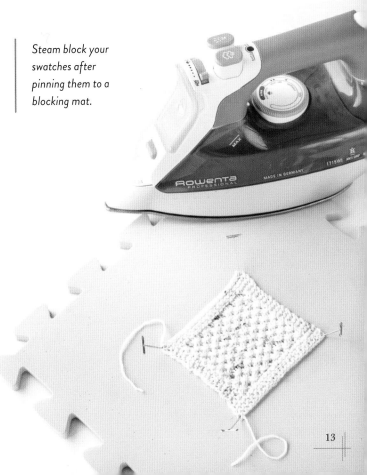

Steam block your swatches after pinning them to a blocking mat.

How does this relate to your finished garment? Pieces knit on wooden needles may be wider and shorter than intended when working strictly by stitch and row counts, and pieces knit on slick metal needles may be more narrow and longer. I don't seem to see much difference in my own knitting, even though I switch between slick wood and slick metal often, but it's something to consider if your gauge is proving problematic.

BINDING OFF

"Bind off loosely in pattern"—it's a phrase I often use in my patterns. To do this, you might use a needle one size up from the one used in the pattern, or you could simply make sure to loosen your tension when binding off.

To bind off in pattern, work the stitches as they present on the row below, then pass the first stitch over the second on the right needle. For example, if you're binding off 1×1 ribbing, k1, p1, pass the first stitch over the second on the RH needle, k1, pass the first stitch over the second, p1, pass the first stitch over the second, and so on.

FINISHING

There are some people who love whipping up the perfect seam, those who think about blocking strategies the moment they cast on their first stitch, and others who loathe the whole lot of it. I fall somewhere in the middle. I try to keep finishing at a minimum for this very reason, but there are some designs that really benefit from being knit in pieces or using a particular finishing technique. Detailed instructions are provided for pieces that call for a specific technique so that your garment will fit properly. If the pattern simply calls for a generic action like "seaming," you may use your preferred method.

Blocking can be done very differently from knitter to knitter, and it's surprisingly personal. It is, however, mandatory. There's no reason to put in hours of knitting just to skip this vital step. Every piece should be washed or steam blocked for several reasons. Natural fiber, whether it's wool or cotton, needs to reset into the new configuration; the garment needs to be shaped carefully to the listed measurements; and many stitch patterns like lace, cables, and select texture stitches must be blocked to lie flat. Gently washing or soaking the pieces allows the fiber to fully relax so that it can be shaped properly. Once dry, stitches are even, the fabric is crisp, and the fit is impeccable.

Wet blocking can be done by spritzing the garment with water and pinning it to blocking mats, or by immersing the garment in water. If you don't have much experience with blocking finished garments, or if you're wondering what the benefits are of the different blocking methods, look no further.

Here's how to wet block:

1. *You can dump just about anything into a tub of lukewarm water, wait for the fibers to become fully saturated, then drain the water and gently press the garment against the side of the tub before carefully transferring it to a towel.*

2. *Roll the towel with the wet garment inside and gently press down on the roll to squeeze out much of the remaining water.*

3. *Transfer the garment to blocking mats, shape the piece to the measurements on the schematic, and use T-pins as needed to hold it in place.*

4. *Let the knitting dry completely before removing the pins.*

I'm a throw-caution-to-the-wind immersion wet blocker. I describe myself this way because if this process isn't handled carefully, some fibers and even stitch patterns can stretch like crazy, and it will be very difficult to undo. Shawls, stoles, most sweaters, and anything that has lace that you want to showcase will transform beautifully using the immersion wet-blocking method. Most people advise against blocking any ribbing this way, but in my opinion, if the ribbing is shaped correctly during blocking, ensuring the rib isn't spread open but rather encouraged to retain its shape for elasticity, there's no reason to avoid it.

Here's how to spray block:

1. *Using a spray bottle filled with cold water, lightly spritz the entire garment.*

2. *Pin the garment to a blocking mat, shaping it carefully to the measurements on the schematic.*

3. *Allow the garment to dry completely before removing the T-pins.*

If a light spritz doesn't allow the fabric to relax as much as desired—either to pin to measurements or to showcase a stitch pattern—continue to spray the garment until the desired result is achieved.

Some fibers respond better to specific blocking methods. A general rule of thumb is that delicate fibers like cashmere and acrylic/wool blends wet-block more effectively with spritzing rather than immersion in a tub. Spritzing is also a great technique for those new to blocking who aren't quite as brazen as I am, or for silk yarns, though opinions are mixed as to whether you should even block silk at all. I, of course, highly recommend it as long as no heat is applied to the silk. No matter which wet-blocking method you choose, make sure your garment is completely dry before removing pins.

Steam blocking is, in my opinion, the absolute best method for blocking alpaca fibers. Alpaca is known for stretching like crazy once knit because the yarn is slippery, has no tooth, and doesn't cling to itself or retain shape because of the natural elasticity of the fiber. I'm unbothered by this stretch if I'm knitting a shawl or stole—something that doesn't need to retain a specific size—but hats, sweaters, or mitts should be steamed. Alpaca is a jerk, and it will eventually lose its shape with enough wear, but steaming can help slow that process (and, in any case, few patterns recommend 100% alpaca). I also steam block small finish details on a garment; for example, button bands.

Here's how to steam block:

1. *Fill your iron with water and set it to the highest steam setting.*

2. *Pin the garment to a blocking mat, shaping it carefully.*

3. *Then slowly steam the fabric with the iron held 1 to 2 inches (2.5–5 cm) away from the surface of the knitting. You'll see the fiber move and even out before your eyes.*

4. *Let the garment cool completely before removing T-pins.*

brioche tips

Even if you've worked brioche many times, there are still moments when you may find yourself looking down at your stitches, wondering what you're doing.

If while working flat in two colors, as for the Idalia project, you set your work down, you may not recall where you left off. You may have a strand of main color on one end and a strand of contrasting color on the other, or both strands on the same end of the work. In either case, look at the stitches along the needle that you worked last. If they're worked in the main color, start with the contrasting color for the next row, and vice versa. Once you know the color you're working with, determine if the stitches facing you are the same color as the working color, in which case you'll be working a "brk" row; if not, it's a "brp" row.

Every season speaks a different language, emits its own odor, and sings its own song.

The capsule wardrobe speaks more about the minds of women today than about their closets.

colorwork tips

One of the most important rules of thumb when it comes to any colorwork is giving the fabric room to breathe. When working floats, separate the stitches on the needles as far as possible between each color change so that the finished fabric will maintain stretch and gauge. This is also true for slipped stitch colorwork, as used in in the Demetria project. Even though only one color is used for each round, there should be plenty of room between the stitches to maintain gauge.

If you've made a mistake in your colorwork, rather than tinking back rows and rows of work, I suggest using the duplicate stitch (see Glossary) to correct mistakes before blocking. To do this, simply use a length of the correct color and a tapestry needle to create the duplicate, then weave in both ends of the yarn.

chapter two

The spring rain,
I definitely saw
The fay of stone.

— MURAKAMI KIJO

Spring

GARTER STITCH & LACE

Depending on where you live, spring temperatures and humidity can range a good deal. While this is generally a wet time when the sun is warm, the air still carries a chill. With fluctuating weather fronts, light layers are a must, and fibers should be wool blends to help you stay warm after a downpour. They also ought to be durable so that they can withstand a variety of wear conditions. (A durable yarn often has some synthetic fiber or mohair blended in for strength; a nice firm twist also helps.) The pieces in this chapter feature garter stitch and lace, using lightweight yarns in luscious wool blends. Mindless garter stitch is the perfect stitch for knitting while out and about, breaking free from the confines of a winter indoors; simple lace adds visual interest and keeps pieces light for those warmer days.

cloria

shawl

Greek; goddess of spring

This large, lacy shawl is the perfect amount of airy and cozy for unpredictable transitional seasons that waver between cool and warm. The center of the shawl is worked in garter stitch, while the sweeping wings are worked in a straightforward eyelet pattern that's easy to execute using the simplest short rows. What makes this piece unique, though, is its collar detail, elevating a simple accessory to a piece that feels more like a garment because it anchors nicely against the body when draped over the shoulders.

Finished Size

About 72" (183 cm) across and 18½" (47 cm) down the center.

Yarn

Fingering weight (#2 Light).

Shown here: Hedgehog Fibres Sock (90% superwash Merino wool, 10% nylon; 437 yd [400 m]/ 3½ oz [100 g]): Pine, 3 hanks.

Needles

Size U.S. 5 (3.75 mm): set of 4 double-pointed (dpns) and 24" (61 cm) circular (cir).

Adjust needle size if necessary to obtain the correct gauge.

Notions

Removable markers (m); cable needle (cn); yarn needle.

Gauge

23 sts and 54 rows = 4" (10 cm) in Garter St.

Notes

— The shawl is worked from the top center down, beginning with the Shawl Center.

— Change to circular needle while working Shawl Center, when dpns are no longer needed. Circular needle is used to accommodate large number of sts. Do not join; work back and forth in rows.

— Wings are formed using simple short-rows, turning, and proceeding as instructed.

— The ribbed collar is worked from picked-up stitches along the center of the shawl, marked on the last row of the shawl center.

Stitch Guide

PICOT BIND-OFF

*Sl 1 st from right needle to left needle, use the knitted method to CO 2 sts (see Glossary), BO 5 sts; rep from * to end.

tab

With dpns, CO 6 sts. Do not join; work back and forth in rows.

Row 1: (WS) K1, p1, k2, p1, k1.

Row 2: Knit.

Rep last 2 rows 3 more times. Do not turn after the last RS row.

Rotate work 45 degrees clockwise, pick up and knit 3 sts along tab edge, rotate work 45 degrees clockwise, pick up and knit 6 sts along CO edge—15 sts.

shawl center

Row 1: (WS) K1, [p1, k2] 4 times, p1, k1.

Row 2: K6, yo, k1, yo, k1 and mark for center st, yo, k1, yo, k6—19 sts.

Row 3: K1, p1, k2, p1, knit to center st, p1, knit to last 5 sts, p1, k2, p1, k1.

Row 4: K6, yo, knit to center st, yo, k1, yo, knit to last 6 sts, yo, k6—4 sts inc'd.

Rep Rows 3 and 4, 68 more times, placing removable markers at the first and last st of the final row—295 sts.

LEFT WING

Short-row 1: (WS) K1, p1, k2, p1, k1, p3, turn.

Short-row 2: (RS) K3, yo, k6—10 sts.

Short-row 3: K1, p1, k2, p1, k1, p6, turn.

Short-row 4: K4, pass third st on RH needle over last 2 sts, yo, k2, yo, k6—13 sts.

Short-row 5: K1, p1, k2, p1, k1, purl to gap, p2, turn—2 sts inc'd.

Short-row 6: K1, *k3, pass third st on RH needle over last 2 sts, yo; rep from * to last 8 sts, k2, yo, k6—1 st inc'd.

Rep Short-rows 5 and 6, 67 more times—217 sts across Left Wing; 365 sts total.

Next row: (WS) K1, p1, k2, p1, k1, purl to center st, p1, purl to last 6 sts, k1, p1, k2, p1, k1.

RIGHT WING

Short-row 1: (RS) K6, yo, k3, turn—10 sts.

Short-row 2: (WS) P4, k1, p1, k2, p1, k1.

Short-row 3: K6, yo, k1, *yo, k3, pass first st on RH needle over last 2 sts; rep from * to gap, k2, turn—3 sts inc'd.

Short-row 4: Purl to last 6 sts, k1, p1, k2, p1, k1.

Rep Short-rows 3 and 4, 68 more times—217 sts across Right Wing; 435 sts total.

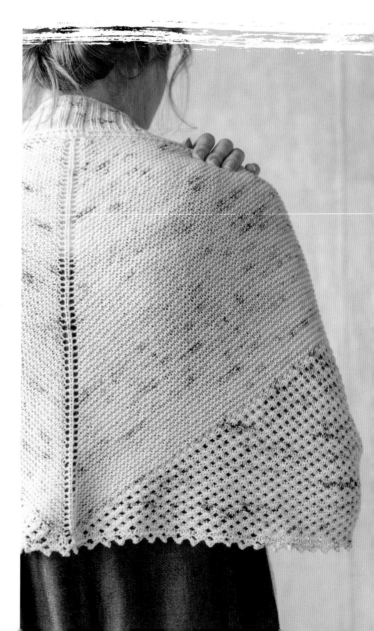

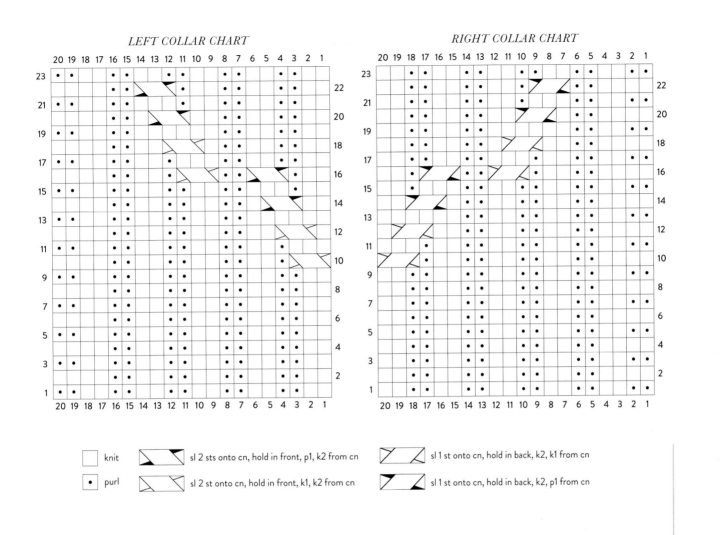

LEFT COLLAR CHART

RIGHT COLLAR CHART

| | | | knit |
| • | | | purl |

slip 2 sts onto cn, hold in front, p1, k2 from cn

slip 2 st onto cn, hold in front, k1, k2 from cn

sl 1 st onto cn, hold in back, k2, k1 from cn

sl 1 st onto cn, hold in back, k2, p1 from cn

border

Row 1: (RS) K6, yo, knit to center st, yo, k1, yo, knit to last 6 sts, yo, k6—439 sts.

Row 2: (WS) K1, p1, k2, p1, knit to last 5 sts, p1, k2, p1, k1.

BO6, work Picot Bind-off (see Stitch Guide) to center st, remove m, BO 1 st, cont in Picot Bind-off to last 6 sts, CO2, BO8.

collar

With RS facing and using removable marker placed on the last row of the Shawl Center as a guide, pick up and knit 214 sts along shawl edge, ending at next removable marker.

Est K2 P2 Rib as follows:

Row 1: (WS) *K2, p2; rep from * to last 2 sts, k2.

Row 2: (RS) K4, *p2, k2; rep from * to last 2 sts, k2.

Rep last 2 rows 3 more times, then rep Row 1 once more.

Est Collar Charts: (RS) Work 20 sts in Right Collar Chart, pm, cont in K2 P2 Rib in patt as est to last 20 sts, pm, work to end in Left Collar Chart.

Work charts and K2 P2 Rib as est through Row 14 of charts.

BO in patt.

finishing

Weave in ends and block to measurements.

harue

vest

Japanese; spring bough

The beauty of this vest lies in its simplicity. Worked flat in a single piece from the bottom up, it has no picked-up stitches or complex shaping, yet the entire piece comes together in the final rows when the front pieces merge at the center back, closing and finishing the garment. Its light weight and casual fit make Harue easy to layer and style for transitional seasons.

Finished Sizes
42 (45¼, 48¾, 52, 55¼, 58¾, 61¼, 64, 68)" (106.5 [115, 124, 132, 140.5, 149, 155.5, 162.5, 172.5] cm) bust circumference.

Designed to fit 32 (35, 38, 41, 44, 47, 50, 53, 56)" (81.5 [89, 96.5, 104, 112, 119.5, 127, 134.5, 142] cm) bust, with 10–12" (25.5–30.5 cm) added for ease.

Vest shown measures 45¼" (115 cm) and fits a 35" (89 cm) bust.

Yarn
Sport weight (#2 Fine).

Shown here: Manos del Uruguay Fino (70% Merino wool, 30% silk; 490 yd [450 m]/3½ oz [100 g]): #SF423 Tincture, 2 (2, 2, 3, 3, 3, 4, 4, 4) hanks.

Needles
Size U.S. 5 (3.75 mm): 24" or 32" (60 or 80 cm) circular (cir).

Adjust needle size if necessary to obtain the correct gauge.

Notions
Markers (m); stitch holders or waste yarn; extra needle for 3-needle Bind-off; yarn needle.

Gauge
24 sts and 40 rows = 4" (10 cm) in Garter St worked flat, blocked.

Notes
⌐ Because Garter Stitch will grow vertically when blocked, ensure accurate measurements by stretching the fabric to the blocked row gauge when knitting the body and for armhole lengths.

⌐ Circular needle is recommended to accommodate large number of sts. Do not join; work back and forth in rows.

body

CO 49 (65, 65, 65, 81, 81, 81, 97, 97) sts, pm, CO 150 (138, 158, 178, 166, 186, 202, 192, 210) sts, pm, CO 49 (65, 65, 65, 81, 81, 81, 97, 97) sts—248 (268, 288, 308, 328, 348, 364, 386, 404) sts. Do not join; work back and forth in rows.

Set-up Row 1: (WS) Work Row 1 of Set-up Chart to m, slm, k13 (2, 7, 12, 1, 6, 10, 1, 4), p1, k2, p1, k1 (0, 1, 0, 1, 0, 0, 0, 0), p2 (0, 2, 0, 2, 0, 0, 0, 0), *k2, p2; rep from * to 18 (8, 12, 18, 6, 12, 16, 7, 10) sts before m, k1 (2, 1, 2, 1, 2, 2, 2, 2), p1, k2, p1, k13 (2, 7, 12, 1, 6, 10, 1, 4), slm, work Row 1 of Set-up Chart to end.

Set-up Row 2: Work Row 2 of Set-up Chart to m, slm, k17 (6, 11, 16, 5, 10, 14, 5, 8), p1 (0, 1, 0, 1, 0, 0, 0, 0), k2 (0, 2, 0, 2, 0, 0, 0, 0), *p2, k2; rep from * to 18 (8, 12, 18, 6, 12, 16, 7, 10) sts before m, p1 (2, 1, 2, 1, 2, 2, 2, 2), knit to m, slm, work Row 2 of Set-up Chart to end.

Set-up Row 3: Rep Set-up Row 1.

Establish pattern as foll:

Row 1: (RS) Work Row 1 of Diamond Lace Chart to m, slm, knit across back to m, slm, work Row 2 of Diamond Lace Chart to end.

Row 2: Work Row 2 of Diamond Lace Chart to m, slm, k13 (2, 7, 12, 1, 6, 10, 1, 4), p1, k2, p1, knit to 17 (6, 11, 16, 5, 10, 14, 5, 8) sts before m, p1, k2, p1, knit to m, slm, work Row 2 of Diamond Lace Chart to end.

Cont as est, working through Row 22 of Diamond Lace Chart, then rep Rows 1–22 for patt until piece meas 11¾ (12, 12¼, 12½, 12½, 12½, 12½, 12½, 12¾)" (30 [30.5, 31, 32, 32, 32, 32, 32, 32.5] cm) from CO edge, ending after a WS row.

DIVIDE FOR RIGHT FRONT

Next Row: (RS) Work in patt as est to m, slm, k12 (1, 6, 11, 0, 5, 9, 0, 3), transfer all rem sts onto st holder or waste yarn and cont working over 61 (66, 71, 76, 81, 86, 90, 97, 100) Right Front sts only.

right front

Work from Diamond Lace Chart in patt until piece meas 7 (7¼, 7½, 7¾, 8, 8¼, 8½, 8¾, 9)" (18 [18.5, 19, 19.5, 20.5, 21, 21.5, 22, 23] cm) from divide, ending after a WS row. Take note of which row of the Diamond Lace Chart was worked last.

Break yarn and place Right Front sts onto st holder or waste yarn.

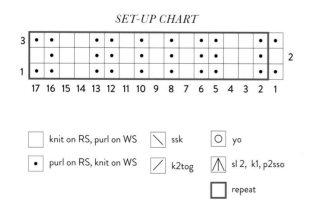

SET-UP CHART

	knit on RS, purl on WS		\	ssk		O	yo
•	purl on RS, knit on WS		/	k2tog		⋀	sl 2, k1, p2sso
							repeat

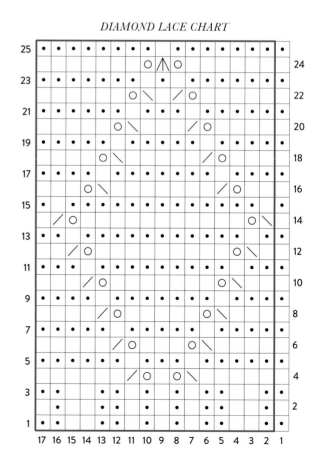

DIAMOND LACE CHART

DIVIDE FOR BACK

Next Row: (RS) Return next 126 (136, 146, 156, 166, 176, 184, 192, 204) held sts to needle for Back. With RS facing, rejoin yarn and knit to 12 (1, 6, 11, 0, 5, 9, 0, 3) sts before m. Keep rem 61 (66, 71, 76, 81, 86, 90, 97, 100) sts on waste yarn for Left Front. Cont working over Back sts only.

back

Next Row: (WS) K1, p1, k2, p1, knit to last 5 sts, p1, k2, p1, k1.

SHAPE ARMHOLES

Dec Row 1: K5, k2tog, knit to last 7 sts, ssk, k5—2 sts dec'd.

Dec Row 2: K1, p1, k2, p1, k2tog, knit to last 7 sts, ssk, p1, k2, p1, k1—2 sts dec'd.

Rep last 2 rows 2 more times—8 sts dec'd; 114 (124, 134, 144, 154, 164, 172, 180, 192) back sts rem.

Next Row: (RS) Knit.

Next Row: (WS) K1, p1, k2, p1, knit to last 5 sts, p1, k2, p1, k1.

Rep last 2 rows until piece meas 7 (7¼, 7½, 7¾, 8, 8¼, 8½, 8¾, 9)" (18 (18.5, 19, 19.5, 20.5, 21, 21.5, 22, 23] cm) from divide, ending after a WS row.

Break yarn and place Back sts onto st holder or waste yarn.

left front

Return 61 (66, 71, 76, 81, 86, 90, 97, 100) held Left Front sts to needle. Rejoin yarn with RS facing and work as for Right Front, being sure to end after the same WS row of the Diamond Lace Chart.

Break yarn. Place Back and Right Front sts onto needle with the Left Front sts.

shape shoulder slope

Set-up Dec Row: (RS) With RS facing, rejoin yarn at Right Front, cont in patt as est to m, slm, knit to end of Right Front, pm, k5 from Back, k2tog, knit to last 7 sts of Back, ssk, k5, pm, knit to m, slm, work across Left Front in patt as est to end—2 sts dec'd; 234 (254, 274, 294, 314, 334, 350, 372, 390) sts; 61 (66, 71, 76, 81, 86, 90, 97, 100) sts each front and 112 (122, 132, 142, 152, 162, 170, 178, 190) sts for Back.

Dec Row 1: (WS) Work across Left Front in patt as est to m, slm, knit to m, slm, k1, p1, k2, p1, k2tog, knit to 7 sts before m, ssk, p1, k2, p1, k1, knit to m, slm, work across Right Front in patt as est to end—2 sts dec'd.

Dec Row 2: Work across Right Front in patt as est to m, slm, knit to m, slm, k5, k2tog, knit to 7 sts before m, ssk, k5, slm, knit to m, slm, work across Left Front in patt as est to end—2 sts dec'd.

Rep the last 2 rows 24 (26, 29, 31, 34, 36, 38, 40, 43) more times—132 (146, 154, 166, 174, 186, 194, 208, 214) sts rem; 61 (66, 71, 76, 81, 86, 90, 97, 100) sts each front and 12 (14, 12, 14, 12, 14, 14, 14, 14) sts for Back.

Sizes 42 (48¾, 55¼)" (106.5 [124, 140.5] cm) Only
Next Row: (WS) Work across Left Front in patt as est to m, slm, knit to m, slm, k1, p1, k2, p2tog, p2tog tbl, k2, p1, k1, slm, knit to m, slm, work across Right Front in patt as est to end—2 sts dec'd; 10 sts rem.

Sizes 45¼ (52, 58¾, 61½, 64, 68)"
(115 [132, 149, 155.5, 162.5, 172.5] cm) Only
Next Row: (WS) Work across Left Front in patt as est to m, slm, knit to m, slm, k1, p1, k2, p3tog, p2tog tbl, k2, p1, k1, slm, knit to m, slm, work across Right Front in patt as est to end—4 sts dec'd; 10 sts rem.

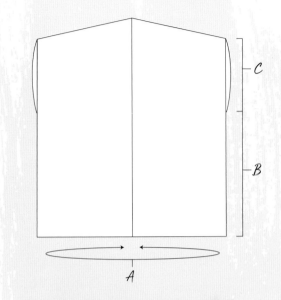

A: 42 (45¼, 48¾, 52, 55¼, 58¾, 61¼, 64, 68)" 106.5 [115, 124, 132, 140.5, 149, 155.5, 162.5, 172.5] cm)

B: 11¾ (12, 12¼, 12½, 12½, 12½, 12½, 12½, 12¾)" 30 [30.5, 31, 32, 32, 32, 32, 32, 32.5] cm)

C: 7 (7¼, 7½, 7¾, 8, 8¼, 8½, 8¾, 9)" 18 (18.5, 19, 19.5, 20.5, 21, 21.5, 22, 23] cm)

finishing

With WS facing each other, arrange sts on needle so that the sts for Left Front and Right Front are held parallel.

Use a spare needle to join Left and Right Front sts using the 3-needle Bind-off method (see Glossary).

Weave in ends and block to measurements.

g e n

tee

Japanese; the origin, source, or spring

Worked from the bottom up in rounds, this simple little pullover is a cinch to knit, with plenty of details to keep the work interesting. The yoke is worked flat in two pieces and joined at the shoulders. I recommend using the 3-needle bind-off for a sturdy shoulder that holds the weight of the sweater, but this is your piece and you may use your preferred method. My short-row shaping, on the other hand, is so easy to execute that fear of short-rows is no reason to avoid this pattern! Gen is the perfect springtime top, easy to style and easy to wear.

Finished Sizes

37¾ (40, 41¾, 44, 45¾, 48, 49¾, 52, 53¾, 56)" (96 [101.5, 106, 112, 116, 122, 126.5, 132, 136.5, 142] cm) bust circumference.

Designed to fit 34 (36, 38, 40, 42, 44, 46, 48, 50, 52)" (86.5 [91.5, 96.5, 101.5, 106.5, 112, 117, 122, 127, 132] cm) bust with about 4" (10 cm) added for ease.

Sweater shown measures 41¾" (106 cm) and fits a 38" (96.5 cm) bust.

Yarn

DK weight (#3 Light).

Shown here: Woolen Boon Boon DK (100% superwash Merino wool; 250 yd [229 m]/4 oz [115 g]): Mint Julep, 3 (4, 4, 4, 4, 4, 5, 5, 5, 5) hanks.

Needles

Size U.S. 7 (4.5 mm): set of 4 or 5 double-pointed (dpn) and 32" (80 cm) circular (cir).

Size U.S. 7 (4.5 mm) crochet hook for reinforced hem.

Adjust needle size if necessary to obtain the correct gauge.

Notions

Markers (m); stitch holders or waste yarn; yarn needle.

Gauge

22 sts and 28 rnds/rows = 4" (10 cm) in St st.

Notes

— This pullover's hem is reinforced with a crochet slip stitch edge. Practice this technique on a swatch before working on the finished piece, since it's made using a crochet hook and may take some practice to obtain even tension.

Stitch Guide

CROCHET HEM

For a sturdy hemline that doesn't curl, stabilize with a crochet slip stitch as foll:

1. Make a slipknot and hold to the back of the work. You'll start between the first and the second st, below a purl bump, as indicated with a contrasting color (*fig. 1*). Insert the crochet hook at that point and pull loop from slipknot through the fabric to front of work (*fig. 2*).

2. *Insert hook into the st below the next purl bump and pull loop through to front of work (*fig. 3*).

3. Loosely pull new st on hook through last st (*fig. 4*).

4. Rep from * to end (*fig. 5*).

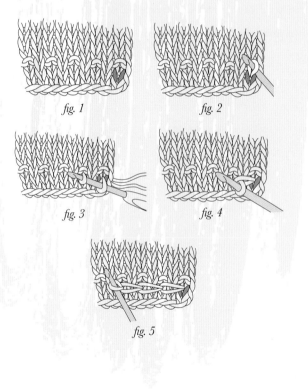

fig. 1

fig. 2

fig. 3

fig. 4

fig. 5

body

With cir needle, CO 208 (220, 230, 242, 252, 264, 274, 286, 296, 308) sts, pm for beg of rnd and join for working in the rnd, being careful not to twist sts.

Knit 2 rnds.

Next Rnd: *K1, p1; rep from * to end.

Work even in St st until piece meas 11¾ (12, 12¼, 12½, 12½, 12½, 12½, 12½, 12½, 12½)" (30 [30.5, 31, 32, 32, 32, 32, 32, 32, 32] cm) from CO.

DIVIDE FOR UNDERARM

K102 (108, 113, 119, 124, 130, 135, 141, 146, 152), place next 4 sts onto st holder or waste yarn for right underarm, place next 100 (106, 111, 117, 122, 128, 133, 139, 144, 150) back sts onto st holder or waste yarn, place next 4 sts onto st holder or waste yarn for left underarm—100 (106, 111, 117, 122, 128, 133, 139, 144, 150) sts rem each Front and Back.

top front

Cont working on Front sts only, working back and forth in rows.

EST NECKLINE PATT

Sizes 37¾ (40, 45¾, 48, 53¾, 56)"
(96 [101.5, 116, 122, 136.5, 142] cm) Only
Row 1: (WS) K1, p48 (51, 59, 62, 70, 73), p2tog, purl to last st, k1—99 (105, 121, 127, 143, 149) sts rem.

Sizes 41¼ (44, 49¾, 52)" (106 [112, 126.5, 132] cm) Only
Row 1: (WS) K1, purl to last st, k1.

All Sizes
Row 2: (RS) K47 (50, 53, 56, 58, 61, 64, 67, 69, 72), k2tog, pm, yo, k1, yo, pm, ssk, k47 (50, 53, 56, 58, 61, 64, 67, 69, 72) to end.

Row 3: K1, purl to m, slm, knit to m, slm, purl to last st, k1.

Row 4: Knit to 2 sts before m, k2tog, slm, yo, knit to m, yo, slm, ssk, knit to end.

Rep last 2 rows until armhole meas 6¼ (6¼, 6½, 6¾, 6¾, 7, 7¼, 7½, 7½, 8)" (16 [16, 16.5, 17, 17, 18, 18.5, 19, 19, 20.5] cm) from underarm, ending after a WS row.

SHAPE SHOULDERS

Short-row 1: (RS) Work in patt as est to last st, turn.

Short-row 2: (WS) Sl1 pwise, work in patt as est to last st, turn.

Short-row 3: Sl1 pwise, work in patt as est to 1 st before gap, turn.

Short-row 4: Sl1 pwise, work in patt as est to 1 st before gap, turn.

Rep last 2 short-rows 9 (9, 10, 10, 11, 11, 11, 12, 13, 14) more times.

Next Row: (RS) Sl1 pwise, work in patt as est to end, closing gaps as you come to them (see Glossary).

Next Row: K1, purl to m, slm, knit to m, slm, purl to last st, closing gaps as you come to them, k1.

Left Front

Row 1: (RS) Work in patt as est over first 37 (39, 42, 43, 45, 47, 50, 53, 55, 58) sts, place next 25 (27, 27, 31, 31, 33, 33, 33, 33, 33) sts onto st holder or waste yarn for neck, place last 37 (39, 42, 43, 45, 47, 50, 53, 55, 58) sts onto st holder or waste yarn for Right Front.

Row 2: Sl1 pwise, work in patt as est to end.

SHAPE NECK

Dec Row: (RS) Work in patt as est to last 3 sts, k2tog, k1—1 st dec'd.

Next Row: Sl1 pwise, work in patt as est to end.

Rep last 2 rows 2 more times—34 (36, 39, 40, 42, 44, 47, 50, 52, 55) sts rem.

Break yarn and place Left Front sts onto st holder or waste yarn.

Right Front

Return 37 (39, 42, 43, 45, 47, 50, 53, 55, 58) held Right Front sts to needle and rejoin yarn with RS facing.

Row 1: (RS) Sl1 pwise, work in patt as est to end.

Row 2: Work in patt as est to end.

SHAPE NECK

Dec Row: (RS) Sl1 pwise, ssk, work in patt as est to end—1 st dec'd.

Next Row: Work in patt as est to end.

Rep last 2 rows 2 more times—34 (36, 39, 40, 42, 44, 47, 50, 52, 55) sts.

Break yarn and place Right Front sts onto st holder or waste yarn.

back

Return 100 (106, 111, 117, 122, 128, 133, 139, 144, 150) held Back sts to needle and rejoin yarn with WS facing. Cont working back and forth in rows as foll:

Row 1: (WS) K1, purl to last st, k1.

Row 2: Knit.

Rep last 2 rows until armhole meas 6¼ (6¼, 6½, 6¾, 6¾, 7, 7¼, 7½, 7½, 8)" (16 [16, 16.5, 17, 17, 18, 18.5, 19, 19, 20.5] cm) from underarm, ending after a WS row.

SHAPE SHOULDERS

Short-row 1: (RS) Work in patt as est to last st, turn.

Short-row 2: (WS) Sl1 pwise, work in patt as est to last st, turn.

Short-row 3: Sl1 pwise, work in patt as est to 1 st before gap, turn.

Short-row 4: Sl1 pwise, work in patt as est to 1 st before gap, turn.

Rep last 2 short-rows 9 (9, 10, 10, 11, 11, 11, 12, 13, 14) more times.

Next Row: (RS) Sl1 pwise, work in patt as est to end, closing gaps as you come to them.

Next Row: K1, purl to m, slm, knit to m, slm, purl to last st, closing gaps as you come to them, k1.

BACK NECK
Est Neckline Patt
Row 1: (RS) K37 (39, 42, 43, 45, 47, 50, 53, 55, 58), pm, k26 (28, 27, 31, 32, 34, 33, 33, 34, 34), pm, k37 (39, 42, 43, 45, 47, 50, 53, 55, 58).

Row 2: K1, purl to m, slm, knit to m, slm, purl to last st, k1.

SHAPE NECK
Dec Row: (RS) Work in patt as est to 2 sts before m, k2tog, slm, knit to m, slm, ssk, knit to end—2 sts dec'd.

Next Row: K1, purl to m, slm, knit to m, slm, purl to last st, k1.

Rep last 2 rows 2 more times—94 (100, 105, 111, 116, 122, 127, 133, 138, 144) sts rem.

Break yarn.

JOIN LEFT SHOULDER
Return 34 (36, 39, 40, 42, 44, 47, 50, 52, 55) held sts from Left Front to shorter cir. Rejoin yarn at left armhole edge, and with WS of Left Front and Back held together, join the 34 (36, 39, 40, 42, 44, 47, 50, 52, 55) shoulder sts using the 3-needle BO method (see Glossary).

JOIN RIGHT SHOULDER
Work the same as the left shoulder, joining yarn at the right neckline and joining to right armhole—26 (28, 27, 31, 32, 34, 33, 33, 34, 34) sts rem for Back neck.

neckband
With RS facing and using dpns, beg at left shoulder, pick up and knit 5 sts along Left Front neckline, k25 (27, 27, 31, 31, 33, 33, 33, 33, 33) held front neck sts, pick up and knit 5 sts along Right Front neckline, k26 (28, 27, 31, 32, 34, 33, 33, 34, 34) back neck sts—61 (65, 64, 72, 73, 77, 76, 76, 77, 77) sts.

BO using Elastic BO method (see Glossary).

sleeves
With RS facing and using dpns, beg at center of underarm, transfer 2 sts held on left onto LH needle, k2, pick up and knit 50 (52, 54, 58, 62, 64, 72, 74, 80, 82) sts evenly around armhole, knit last 2 held sts from underarm, pm, join for rnds—54 (56, 58, 62, 66, 68, 76, 78, 84, 86) sts.

Knit 1 rnd.

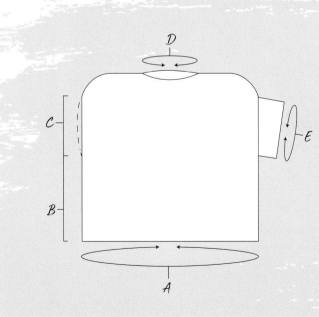

A: 37¾ (40, 41¾, 44, 45¾, 48, 49¾, 52, 53¾, 56)"
96 [101.5, 106, 112, 116, 122, 126.5, 132, 136.5, 142] cm)

B: 11¾ (12, 12¼, 12½, 12½, 12½, 12½, 12½, 12½, 12½)"
30 [30.5, 31, 32, 32, 32, 32, 32, 32, 32] cm)

C: 7¾ (7¾, 8, 8¼, 8¼, 8½, 8¾, 9, 9, 9½)"
19.5 [19.5, 20.5, 21, 21, 21.5, 22, 23, 23, 24] cm)

D: 11 (11¾, 11¾, 13, 13¼, 14, 13¾, 13¾, 14, 14)"
28 [30, 30, 33, 33.5, 35.5, 35, 35, 35.5, 35.5] cm)

E: 9¾ (10¼, 10½, 11¼, 12, 12¼, 13¾, 14¼, 15¼, 15¾)"
25 [26, 26.5, 28.5, 30.5, 31, 35, 36, 38.5, 40] cm)

SHAPE CAP

Short-row 1: K38 (40, 42, 46, 50, 52, 60, 62, 68, 70), turn.

Short-row 2: Sl1 pwise, p21 (23, 25, 29, 33, 35, 43, 45, 51, 53), turn.

Short-row 3: Sl1 pwise, knit to 1 st before gap, close gap, k3, turn.

Short-row 4: Sl1 pwise, purl to 1 st before gap, close gap, p3, turn.

Rep last 2 short-rows once more.

Next Row: Sl1 pwise, knit to end, closing rem gap as you come to it.

Rnd 1: Knit to gap, transfer next st onto RH needle, lift the st positioned around the st with the LH needle and place onto the RH needle, transfer both sts back to the LH needle and knit them together tbl, knit to end.

Knit 1 rnd.

EST WIDE EYELET

Rnd 1: K3 (0, 1, 3, 1, 2, 2, 3, 2, 3), *[k2tog] twice, [yo] twice, [ssk] twice; rep from * to last 3 (0, 1, 3, 1, 2, 2, 3, 2, 3) st(s), knit to end—42 (42, 44, 48, 50, 52, 58, 60, 64, 66) sts rem.

Rnd 2: K3 (0, 1, 3, 1, 2, 2, 3, 2, 3), *k2tog, [k1, p1] 3 times into double yo, ssk; rep from * to last 3 (0, 1, 3, 1, 2, 2, 3, 2, 3) st(s), knit to end—54 (56, 58, 62, 66, 68, 76, 78, 84, 86) sts.

Rnd 3: K4 (1, 2, 4, 2, 3, 3, 4, 3, 4), *k6, k2tog leaving sts on LH needle, then knit into the first st of k2tog once more; rep from * to last 10 (7, 8, 10, 8, 9, 9, 10, 9, 10) sts, knit to end.

Knit 6 rnds.

Next Rnd: *K1, p1; rep from * to end.

Knit 1 rnd.

BO all sts.

finishing

Using crochet hook, work Crochet Hem (see Stitch Guide) around the lower edge of the body.

Weave in ends and block to measurements.

woolen

boon

When selecting yarns for this collection, one of the many boxes I was looking to tick was finding companies founded by or run by women, but also independents that aren't necessarily mainstream. This interested me because, years ago, when putting together a game plan for making money and staying home with my daughters, I pursued many avenues before finding my niche in design, so I have a keen insight on just how much time and dedication these women are putting into their work.

Woolen Boon was one of those yarns that I discovered while scrolling Instagram, drawn to Sonya Brazell's products—she's the founder of the company—because of the variety of colors and techniques she uses on her bases. It just so happened that her Mint Julep colorway was perfectly matched to my color inspiration for the spring chapter.

A bit more about Sonya and her mom-and-pop company:

The company started out small, with Sonya carrying most of the weight before roping in her husband, Ryan, to work for her. This loving partnership created a sturdy foundation upon which to erect the Woolen Boon brand. The couple and the company made a huge change, moving from New Hampshire to Austin, Texas, in 2018, and quickly set up shop to keep up with the demands of their stock lists around the U.S., along with a few international locations.

One of the qualities that sets Woolen Boon yarns apart from other dye companies is that Sonya and Ryan created a system for addressing the "problematic" colorways so common in many hand-dyed artisan yarns: They label colors as "cousins" or "sisters." Cousins are wild and painterly; they can vary greatly in finished look from skein to skein, even when the recipe is repeated exactly. This gives the knitter a clue that he or she must alternate skeins when working larger projects or else expect a lot of variation. Sisters are more closely related—not twins—but the color patterning is more regular, with less variation.

Woolen Boon is a fast-growing company that sources ethically produced fibers, has a strong foundation in family, and has a great sense of humor apparent on their website, but takes making beautiful yarns seriously.

WHY BOON DK?

The yarn base is perfectly round and balanced, a slightly heavy DK that works up very quickly and is so smooth that the process of sliding it across the needles is sensational. In addition to the satisfying sensation of knitting with soft, noodly strands, the color is layered artfully so that each stitch has a speck or splash of surprise. It's one of those inherently difficult things to describe if you've never gotten your hands on a small-batch hand-dye. Even though Gen has details and modern shaping that create interest both for the knitter and the wearer, the yarn plays the starring role. Not every piece is well suited to a yarn that dominates, but Gen was the perfect canvas for the painterly quality of Mint Julep.

y a m k a

boatneck

Hopi; blossom

This simple little pullover is one of those easy-to-wear pieces that can be styled many ways, which I love for transitional seasons. The pullover is worked in rounds from the bottom up before splitting for the front and back. The stitches are simple to execute and there is very little shaping, so this pattern is appropriate for knitters having a variety of skill levels. Small details are the focus, so you'll be introduced to a stretchy 3-needle bind-off that will be an invaluable skill for any knitter who loves bottom-up sweaters as much as I do.

Finished Sizes
30¾ (34¾, 38½, 42¼, 46¼, 50, 54, 57¾)" (78 [88.5, 98, 107.5, 117.5, 127, 137, 146.5] cm) bust circumference.

Designed to fit 28¼ (32¼, 36, 39¾, 43¾, 47½, 51½, 55¼)" (72 [82, 91.5, 101, 111, 120.5, 131, 140.5] cm) bust with 2.5" (6.5 cm) added for ease.

Sweater shown measures 38½" (98 cm) and fits a 36" (91.5 cm) bust.

Yarn
Fingering weight (#1 Super Fine).

Shown here: Magpie Fibers Solo Fingering (100% superwash Merino wool; 434 yd [397 m]/4 oz [115 g]): Ghost Town, 2 (2, 2, 3, 3, 4, 4, 5) hanks.

Needles
All ribbing: Size U.S. 4 (3.5 mm): set of 4 or 5 double-pointed (dpn) and 24" or 32" (60 or 80 cm) circular (cir).

Body: Size U.S. 5 (3.75 mm): 24" or 32" (60 or 80 cm) circular (cir).

Adjust needle size if necessary to obtain the correct gauge.

Notions
Markers (m); stitch holders or waste yarn; extra needle for 3-needle Bind-off; yarn needle.

Gauge
27 sts and 44 rnds/rows = 4" (10 cm) in Garter Slip St worked in rnds on larger needles.

Notes
⁓ This piece is worked seamlessly from the bottom up, and shoulders are joined before sleeves are picked up and knit from the armholes. This construction results in minimal finishing.

Stitch Guide

1×1 RIBBING

Worked in Rnds (multiple of 2 sts)

Rnd 1: *K1, p1; rep from * to end.

Rep Rnd 1 for patt.

Worked in Rows (multiple of 2 sts + 1)

Row 1: (RS) K2, *p1, k1; rep from * to last st, k1.

Row 2: (WS) *K1, p1; rep from * to last st, k1.

Rep Rows 1 and 2 for patt.

GARTER SLIP STITCH (MULTIPLE OF 13 STS)

Worked in Rnds

Rnd 1: P6, *sl1 pwise wyb, p12; rep from * to last 7 sts, sl1 pwise wyb, p6.

Rnd 2: Knit.

Rep Rnds 1 and 2 for patt.

Worked in Rows

Row 1: (WS) K6, *sl1 pwise wyif, k12; rep from * to last 7 sts, sl1 pwise wyif, k6.

Row 2: (RS) Knit.

Rep Rows 1 and 2 for patt.

STRETCHY 3-NEEDLE BIND-OFF

1. Holding needles parallel with WS together and using a third needle to work sts (*fig. 1*), knit the first stitch on each needle together.

2. * Reverse yo by bringing yarn around the RH needle from back to front (*fig. 2*).

3. Knit the next st on each needle together—3 sts on RH needle (*fig. 3*).

4. Pass the first st and yo over the second st on the RH needle (*fig. 4*). Rep from * until all sts are BO.

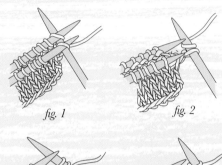
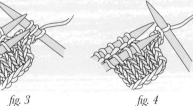

fig. 1   *fig. 2*

fig. 3   *fig. 4*

body

With smaller cir, CO 208 (234, 260, 286, 312, 338, 364, 390) sts. Pm for beg of rnd and join for working in the rnd, being careful not to twist sts.

Work 1×1 Ribbing (see Stitch Guide) until piece meas 1" (2.5 cm) from CO edge.

Knit 2 rnds even.

Change to larger cir.

Work in Garter Slip St (see Stitch Guide) until piece meas 12¾ (13, 13¼, 13½, 13½, 13½, 14, 14)" (32.5 [33, 33.5, 34.5, 34.5, 34.5, 35.5, 35.5] cm) from CO edge, ending after Rnd 2 of patt.

DIVIDE BACK AND FRONT

Place first 104 (117, 130, 143, 156, 169, 182, 195) sts from next rnd onto st holder or waste yarn and turn work to beg a WS row. Cont working back and forth in rows on 104 (117, 130, 143, 156, 169, 182, 195) Front sts only.

front

Cont working Garter Slip St in rows until armhole meas 4 (4¼, 4½, 4¾, 5¼, 5½, 6, 6¼)" (10 [11, 11.5, 12, 13.5, 14, 15, 16] cm), ending after a WS row.

SET UP LACE INSERT

Sizes 30¾ (42¼, 54)" (78 [107.5, 137] cm) Only
Inc Row: (RS) K33, pm, k19 (38, 58), M1, k19 (39, 58), pm, k33—105 (144, 183) sts.

Sizes 34¾ (46¼, 57¾)" (88.5 [117.5, 146.5] cm) Only
Next Row: (RS) K33, pm, knit to last 33 sts, pm, k33.

Sizes 38½ (50)" (98 [127] cm) Only
Inc Row: (RS) K33, pm, [k21 (34), M1] 2 times, k22 (35), pm, k33—132 (171) sts.

All Sizes
Next Row: (WS) Work in Garter Slip St as est to m, slm, purl to m, slm, work in Garter Slip St as est to end.

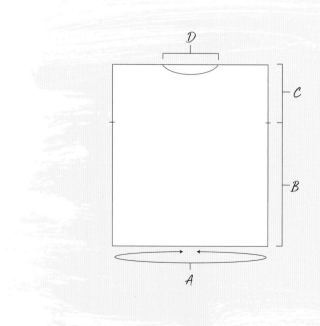

A: 30¾ (34¾, 38½, 42¼, 46¼, 50, 54, 57¾)"
(78 [88.5, 98, 107.5, 117.5, 127, 137, 146.5] cm)

B: 12¾ (13, 13¼, 13½, 13½, 13½, 14, 14)"
(32.5 [33, 33.5, 34.5, 34.5, 34.5, 35.5, 35.5] cm)

C: 6½ (6¾, 7, 7¼, 7¾, 8, 8½, 8¾)"
(16.5 [17, 18, 18.5, 19.5, 20.5, 21.5, 22] cm)

D: 5½ (5¾, 6¼, 6¾, 6¾, 7¼, 7¼, 7½)"
(14 [14.5, 16, 17, 17, 18.5, 18.5, 19] cm)

EST LACE INSERT PATT

Row 1: (RS) Work in Garter Slip St as est to m, slm, yo, *sl2, k1, p2sso, [yo] twice; rep from * to 3 sts before m, sl2, k1, p2sso, yo, slm, work in Garter Slip St as est to end.

Row 2: (WS) Work in Garter Slip St as est to m, slm, p2, *purl into the first yo, knit into the second yo, p1; rep from * to 1 st before m, p1, slm, work in Garter Slip St as est to end.

Rep last 2 rows 5 more times.

Knit 1 RS row, removing markers as you come to them.

Sizes 30¾ (34¾, 50, 54, 57¾)" (78 [88.5, 127, 137, 146.5] cm) Only
Next Row: (WS) K1, purl to last st, k1.

Sizes 38½ (42¼, 46¼)" (98 [107.5, 117.5] cm) Only
Dec Row: (WS) K1, p64 (70, 76), p2tog, purl to last st, k1—131 (143, 155) sts.

All Sizes
Change to smaller cir. Do not join; work back and forth in rows.

Work in 1×1 Ribbing for 1" (2.5 cm), ending after a RS row.

SHAPE NECK

Next Row: (WS) Work in ribbing as est over first 34 (39, 44, 49, 55, 61, 67, 72) sts, BO 37 (39, 43, 45, 45, 49, 49, 51) sts loosely in patt, work in ribbing as est to end—34 (39, 44, 49, 55, 61, 67, 72) sts rem on each side for shoulders.

Break yarn and place rem sts onto st holder or waste yarn.

back

Return 104 (117, 130, 143, 156, 169, 182, 195) held back sts to larger cir.

With WS facing, rejoin yarn and cont working Garter Slip St back and forth in rows until armhole meas 5½ (5¾, 6, 6¼, 6¾, 7, 7½, 7¾)" (14 [14.5, 15, 16, 17, 18, 19, 19.5] cm) from divide, ending after a WS row.

Next Row: (RS) Knit.

Sizes 30¾ (38½, 54)" (78 [98, 137] cm) Only
Inc Row: (WS) K1, p52 (65, 91), M1P, purl to last st, k1—105 (131, 183) sts.

Sizes 34¾ (42¼, 57¾)" (88.5 [107.5, 146.5] cm) Only
Next Row: (WS) K1, purl to last st, k1.

Size 46¼" (117.5 cm) Only
Dec Row: (WS) K1, p76, p2tog, purl to last st, k1—155 sts.

Size 50" (127 cm) Only
Inc Row: (WS) K1, [p56, M1] 2 times, purl to last st, k1—171 sts.

All Sizes
Change to smaller cir. Do not join; work back and forth in rows.

Work in 1×1 Ribbing for 1" (2.5 cm), ending after a RS row.

SHAPE NECK

Next Row: (WS) Work in ribbing as est over first 34 (39, 44, 49, 55, 61, 67, 72) sts, BO 37 (39, 43, 45, 45, 49, 49, 51) sts loosely in patt, work in ribbing as est to end—34 (39, 44, 49, 55, 61, 67, 72) sts rem on each side for shoulders. Do not break yarn.

JOIN SHOULDERS

Return 34 (39, 44, 49, 55, 61, 67, 72) held sts from Right Front to needle and with WS held together, and Back RS facing, work Stretchy 3-needle Bind-off (see Stitch Guide) over right shoulder, working from armhole to neck opening. Break yarn.

Return 34 (39, 44, 49, 55, 61, 67, 72) held sts from Left Front to needle and join the same as the right shoulder, working from neck opening to armhole. Break yarn.

finishing
ARMHOLE EDGING

With dpns and RS facing, beg at underarm, pick up and knit 90 (92, 94, 98, 102, 106, 110, 114) sts evenly around armhole. Pm for beg of rnd and join for working in rnds.

Work 1×1 Ribbing for 4 rnds.

BO loosely in patt.

Weave in ends and lightly block to measurements.

akina

tunic

Japanese; bright spring flower

Everything spring is wrapped up in this tunic-length pullover. Worked from the bottom up and featuring a simple lace body, it then continues to the garter stitch top with sloped shoulders. Shoulders are seamed and sleeve stitches are picked up and knit from the armholes, dotted with a simple lace pattern reminiscent of flower buds or pine cones. Sleeves and neckline are all finished in a clean I-cord bind-off. The kimono-style sleeves are probably my favorite feature of the design—both breezy and cozy, they elevate the simple silhouette to something striking and modern.

Finished Sizes

32 (34¼, 36¼, 39, 41, 43¼, 45½, 48, 50¼)" (81.5 [87, 92, 99, 104, 110, 115.5, 122, 127.5] cm) bust circumference.

Designed to fit 30¾ (33, 35, 37¾, 39¾, 42, 44¼, 46¾, 49)" (78 [84, 89, 96, 101, 106.5, 112.5, 118.5, 124.5] cm) bust, with 1¼" (3 cm) added for ease.

Sweater shown measures 36¼" (92 cm) and fits a 35" (89 cm) bust.

Yarn

DK weight (#3 Light).

Shown here: Hazel Knits Lively DK (90% superwash Merino wool, 10% nylon; 275 yd

[251.5 m]/3½ oz [100 g]): Conch, 5 (5, 6, 6, 6, 7, 7, 7, 8) hanks.

Needles

Size U.S. 6 (4 mm): 24" (60 cm) and 16" (40 cm) circular (cir).

Adjust needle size if necessary to obtain the correct gauge.

Notions

Marker (m); stitch holders or waste yarn; yarn needle.

Gauge

22 sts and 34 rnds/rows = 4" (10 cm) in Garter St; 24 sts and 30 rnds = 4" (10 cm) in Lace patt.

Notes

⟶ This piece is worked in rounds from the bottom up, and cast on using the Channel Island Cast-on method (see Glossary). This method requires a tail that should measure about 1" (2.5 cm) for each stitch cast on. Use this method to cast on your gauge swatch so that you're familiar with it when it comes time to knit the garment.

⟶ When measuring the Garter St, do so with the garment hanging. The added weight will give a more accurate measurement.

Stitch Guide

LACE EDGE (MULTIPLE OF 12 STS)

Rnd 1: *K1, yo, k4, sl2, k1, p2sso, k4, yo; rep from * to end.

Rnd 2 and All Even-numbered Rnds: Knit.

Rnd 3: *K2, yo, k3, sl2, k1, p2sso, k3, yo, k1; rep from * to end.

Rnd 5: *K1, yo, ssk, yo, k2, sl2, k1, p2sso, k2, yo, k2tog, yo; rep from * to end.

Rnd 7: *K2, yo, ssk, yo, k1, sl2, k1, p2sso, k1, yo, k2tog, yo, k1; rep from * to end.

Rnd 9: *K3, yo, ssk, yo, sl2, k1, p2sso, yo, k2tog, yo, k2; rep from * to end.

Rnd 11: *K4, yo, ssk, k1, k2tog, yo, k3; rep from * to end.

Rnd 13: *K5, yo, sl2, k1, p2sso, yo, k4; rep from * to end.

Rnd 14: Knit.

Work Rnds 1–12, then rep Rnds 13 and 14 for patt.

LACE EDGE CHART

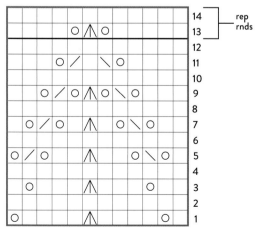

SHOULDER SEAM

Shoulder seams are worked with RS facing and with bound-off edges held horizontally with one as a bottom row and the other as a top row.

Seam as foll:

fig. 1

fig. 2

fig. 3

1. Insert threaded tapestry needle into the outside leg of the first stitch on the bottom row, then into the outside leg of the first stitch on the top row (*fig. 1*).

2. *Insert tapestry needle into the outside leg of the next stitch on the top row, then once again into the outside leg of the first stitch on the bottom row (*fig. 2*).

3. Insert the tapestry needle into the outside leg of the next stitch on the bottom row, then once again into the outside leg of the second stitch on the top row (*fig. 3*). Rep from * until all stitches are seamed.

LITTLE PINE CONE LACE
(MULTIPLE OF 18 STS + 10)

Rnd 1 and All Odd-Numbered Rnds: Knit.

Rnd 2: Yo, p3, sl2, k1, p2sso, p3, yo, *k9, yo, p3, sl2, k1, p2sso, p3, yo; rep from * to last st, k1.

Rnd 4: K1, yo, p2, sl2, k1, p2sso, p2, yo, *k11, yo, p2, sl2, k1, p2sso, p2, yo; rep from * to last 2 sts, knit to end.

Rnd 6: K2, yo, p1, sl2, k1, p2sso, p1, yo, *k13, yo, p1, sl2, k1, p2sso, p1, yo; rep from * to last 3 sts, knit to end.

Rnd 8: K3, yo, sl2, k1, p2sso, yo, *k15, yo, sl1, k1, p2sso, yo; rep from * to last 4 sts, knit to end.

Rnd 10: K9, *yo, p3, sl2, k1, p2sso, p3, yo, k9; rep from * to last st, k1.

Rnd 12: K10, *yo, p2, sl2, k1, p2sso, p2, yo, k11; rep from * to end.

Rnd 14: K10, *k1, yo, p1, sl2, k1, p2sso, p1, yo, k12; rep from * to end.

Rnd 16: K10, *k2, yo, sl2, k1, p2sso, yo, k13; rep from * to end.

Rep Rnds 1–16 for patt.

LITTLE PINE CONE LACE CHART

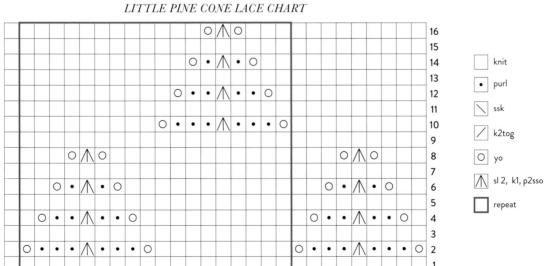

□ knit

• purl

╲ ssk

╱ k2tog

○ yo

⋀ sl 2, k1, p2sso

☐ repeat

body

Using Channel Island Cast-on (see Glossary) and longer needles, CO 192 (204, 216, 228, 240, 252, 264, 276, 288) sts, pm and join for rnds.

Work Lace Edge (see Stitch Guide), working Rnds 1–13 once, then rep Rnds 12 and 13 until piece meas 9½" (24 cm) from CO edge.

Knit 1 rnd.

Dec Rnd: [K10 (10, 11, 14, 15, 16, 16, 21, 22), k2tog] 16 (16, 16, 14, 14, 14, 14, 12, 12) times, knit to end—176 (188, 200, 214, 226, 238, 250, 264, 276) sts.

Purl 1 rnd.

Beg working Garter St in rnds (see Glossary) until piece meas 4 (4¼, 4½, 4¾, 4¾, 4¾, 4¾, 4¾, 4¾)" (10 [11, 11.5, 12, 12, 12, 12, 12, 12] cm from dec rnd, ending after a purl rnd.

DIVIDE FRONT AND BACK

Next Rnd: K5, place last 5 sts onto st holder or waste yarn, k78 (84, 90, 97, 103, 109, 115, 122, 128) sts for Front, k5, pm, k5, place last 10 sts onto st holder or waste yarn with marker in place, k83 (89, 95, 102, 108, 114, 120, 127, 133) sts for Back to end, pm, and place last 5 sts onto st holder or waste yarn—78 (84, 90, 97, 103, 109, 115, 122, 128) sts rem each Front and Back. Transfer Back sts onto a separate st holder or waste yarn. Break yarn. Cont working back and forth in rows on Front sts only.

front

Rejoin yarn with WS facing and cont working in Garter St, back and forth in rows (see Glossary), until armhole meas 5¾ (6, 6¼, 6½, 6½, 6¾, 7¼, 7¼, 7½)" (14.5 [15, 16, 16.5, 16.5, 17, 18.5, 18.5, 19] cm) from divide, ending after a WS row.

Next Row: (RS) K48 (52, 55, 61, 64, 68, 71, 75, 79), place last 18 (20, 20, 25, 25, 27, 27, 28, 30) sts onto a st holder or waste yarn for neck, knit to end—30 (32, 35, 36, 39, 41, 44, 47, 49) sts rem on each side. Cont working on Right Front sts only, leaving the Left Front sts on needle to be worked later.

SHAPE RIGHT FRONT NECK

Next Row: (WS) Knit.

Dec Row: (RS) K1, ssk, knit to end—1 st dec'd.

Rep the last 2 rows 4 more times—25 (27, 30, 31, 34, 36, 39, 42, 44) sts rem.

Work even in Garter St until armhole meas 7¾ (8, 8¼, 8½, 8½, 8¾, 9¼, 9¼, 9½)" (19.5 [20.5, 21, 21.5, 21.5, 22, 23.5, 23.5, 24] cm) from divide, ending after a RS row.

Shape Right Front Shoulder

Row 1: (WS) BO 3 (4, 4, 4, 5, 6, 6, 7, 7) sts, knit to end—22 (23, 26, 27, 29, 30, 33, 35, 37) sts rem.

Row 2: Knit.

Rows 3 and 4: Rep Rows 1 and 2—19 (19, 22, 23, 24, 24, 27, 28, 30) sts rem.

Row 5: (WS) BO 3 (3, 4, 4, 5, 5, 6, 7, 7) sts, knit to end—16 (16, 18, 19, 19, 19, 21, 21, 23) sts rem.

Row 6: Knit.

With RS facing, BO all sts knitwise. Break yarn.

SHAPE LEFT FRONT NECK

Reattach yarn to the neck edge of the rem Left Front sts to beg working a WS row.

Next Row: (WS) Knit.

Dec Row: (RS) Knit to last 3 sts, k2tog, k1—1 st dec'd.

Rep the last 2 rows 4 more times—25 (27, 30, 31, 34, 36, 39, 42, 44) sts rem.

Work even in Garter St until armhole meas 7¾ (8, 8¼, 8½, 8½, 8¾, 9¼, 9¼, 9½)" (19.5 [20.5, 21, 21.5, 21.5, 22, 23.5, 23.5, 24] cm) from divide, ending after a RS row.

Shape Left Front Shoulder

Row 1: (WS) Knit.

Row 2: BO 3 (4, 4, 4, 5, 6, 6, 7, 7) sts, knit to end—22 (23, 26, 27, 29, 30, 33, 35, 37) sts rem.

Rows 3–5: Rep Rows 1 and 2 once, then rep Row 1 once more—19 (19, 22, 23, 24, 24, 27, 28, 30) sts rem.

Row 6: BO 3 (3, 4, 4, 5, 5, 6, 7, 7) sts, knit to end—16 (16, 18, 19, 19, 19, 21, 21, 23) sts rem.

With WS facing, BO all sts knitwise. Break yarn.

back

Return 78 (84, 90, 97, 103, 109, 115, 122, 128) held back sts to needles and rejoin yarn with WS facing.

Work Garter St back and forth in rows until armhole meas 7 (7¼, 7½, 7¾, 7¾, 8, 8½, 8½, 8¾)" (18 [18.5, 19, 19.5, 19.5, 20.5, 21.5, 21.5, 22] cm) from divide, ending after a WS row.

Next Row: (RS) K39 (42, 45, 48, 51, 55, 58, 61, 64), pm, k9 (10, 10, 13, 13, 14, 14, 14, 15), place last 18 (20, 20, 25, 25, 27, 27, 28, 30) sts and marker onto st holder or waste yarn for neck, knit to end—30 (32, 35, 36, 39, 41, 44, 47, 49) sts rem each side. Cont working on Left Back sts only, leaving the Right Back sts on needle to be worked later.

SHAPE LEFT BACK NECK
Next Row: (WS) Knit.

Dec Row: (RS) K1, ssk, knit to end—1 st dec'd.

Rep the last 2 rows 4 more times—25 (27, 30, 31, 34, 36, 39, 42, 44) sts rem.

Shape Left Back Shoulder

Row 1: (WS) BO 3 (4, 4, 4, 5, 6, 6, 7, 7) sts, knit to end—22 (23, 26, 27, 29, 30, 33, 35, 37) sts rem.

Row 2: Knit.

Rows 3 and 4: Rep Rows 1 and 2—19 (19, 22, 23, 24, 24, 27, 28, 30) sts rem.

Row 5: BO 3 (3, 4, 4, 5, 5, 6, 7, 7) sts, knit to end—16 (16, 18, 19, 19, 19, 21, 21, 23) sts rem.

Row 6: Knit 1 row.

With WS facing, BO all sts knitwise. Break yarn, leaving a 15″ (38 cm) tail.

SHAPE RIGHT BACK NECK

Reattach yarn to the neck edge of the Right Back sts to beg working a WS row.

Next Row: (WS) Knit.

Dec Row: (RS) Knit to last 3 sts, k2tog, k1—1 st dec'd.

Rep the last 2 rows 4 more times—25 (27, 30, 31, 34, 36, 39, 42, 44) sts rem.

Shape Right Back Shoulder

Row 1: (WS) Knit.

Row 2: BO 3 (4, 4, 5, 6, 6, 6, 7, 7) sts, knit to end—22 (23, 26, 27, 29, 30, 33, 35, 37) sts rem.

Rows 3–5: Rep Rows 1 and 2 once, then rep Row 1 once more—19 (19, 22, 23, 24, 24, 27, 28, 30) sts rem.

Row 6: BO 3 (3, 4, 4, 5, 5, 6, 7, 7) sts, knit to end—16 (16, 18, 19, 19, 19, 21, 21, 23) sts rem.

Row 7: Knit.

With RS facing, BO all sts. Break yarn, leaving a 15″ (38 cm) tail.

JOIN SHOULDERS

Using the yarn tails and a tapestry needle, seam Front and Back shoulders (see Stitch Guide).

sleeves

With RS facing and using shorter needles, transfer the 5 underarm sts left of the marker to needles, k5, pick up and knit 92 (96, 98, 100, 100, 102, 108, 108, 119) sts evenly around armhole, transfer the 5 underarm sts right of the marker to needles, k5, pm, and join for working in the rnd—102 (106, 108, 110, 110, 112, 118, 118, 120) sts.

EST LITTLE PINE CONE LACE PATT

Next Rnd: K1 (3, 4, 5, 5, 6, 0, 0, 1), work Little Pine Cone Lace (see Stitch Guide) to last 1 (3, 4, 5, 5, 6, 0, 0, 1) st(s).

Cont working Little Pine Cone Lace as est until Rnds 1–16 have been completed 3 times.

Knit 2 rnds.

Purl 1 rnd.

BO using I-cord Bind-off (see Glossary).

neckband

With RS facing and using shorter needles, transfer 9 (10, 10, 13, 13, 14, 14, 14, 15) Back neck sts left of the marker to needles and knit across, pick up and knit 9 sts along Back neck edge, pick up and knit 14 sts along Front neck edge, transfer 18 (20, 20, 25, 25, 27, 27, 28, 30) Front neck sts to needles and knit across, pick up and knit 14 sts along Front neck edge, pick up and knit 9 sts along Back neck edge, transfer rem 9 (10, 10, 12, 12, 13, 13, 14, 15) Back neck sts right of the marker to needles, knit to marker—82 (86, 86, 96, 96, 100, 100, 102, 106) sts.

Purl 1 rnd.

BO using I-cord Bind-off.

finishing

Weave in ends. Block to measurements.

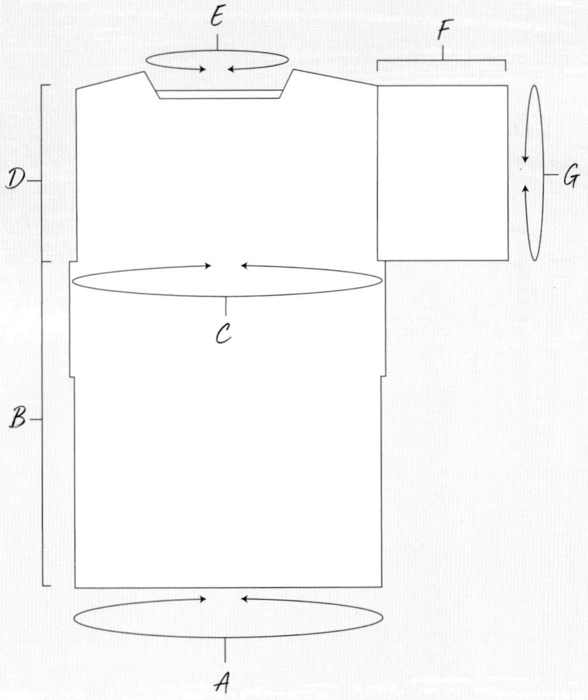

A: 32 (34, 36, 38, 40, 42, 44, 46, 48)" (81.5 [86.5, 91.5, 96.5, 101.5, 106.5, 112, 117, 122] cm)

B: 13¾ (14¼, 14½, 15, 15, 15¼, 15¼, 15½, 15½)" (35 [36, 37, 38, 38, 38.5, 38.5, 39.5, 39.5] cm)

C: 32 (34¼, 36¼, 39, 41, 43¼, 45½, 48, 50¼)" (81.5 [87, 92, 99, 104, 110, 115.5, 122, 127.5] cm)

D: 7¾ (8, 8¼, 8½, 8½, 8¾, 9¼, 9¼, 9½)" (19.5 [20.5, 21, 21.5, 21.5, 22, 23.5, 23.5, 24] cm)

E: 15 (15¾, 15¾, 17½, 17½, 18¼, 18¼, 18½, 19¼)" (38 [40, 40, 44.5, 44.5, 46.5, 46.5, 47, 49] cm)

F: 6¾" (17 cm)

G: 18½ (19¼, 19¾, 20, 20, 20¼, 21½, 21½, 23½)" (47 [49, 50, 51, 51, 51.5, 54.5, 54.5, 59.5] cm)

chapter three

The cicada finally,
In the gale,
Cease his voice.
—YAMAGUCHI SEISHI

Summer

COLOR ACCENTS

I've always understood the reason for putting down the needles during the hot summer months, when tending gardens and reexperiencing the world full-body becomes possible for a great many of us, briefly. However, I find that my hands still itch to move in the evenings, when the sun has finally settled and late-night silence graces the house. Fibers must be light and smooth to both knit and wear during this season, and it's the perfect time for easy knitting with some creative color play. These pieces are designed with hot, humid air in mind and feature breathable plant fibers—cotton and linen—with interesting color accents.

s o l a n g e
stole

French; patron saint of rain

This wrap features two different lace patterns and is worked end to end. The sides are picked up and knit in contrasting-color ribbing for a stunning finish. Solange is the perfect accessory for warm weather or cool summer nights, even in humid climates. The suggested yarn is perfectly soft against the skin, balanced and round for exceptional stitch definition.

Finished Size
58½" (148.5 cm) long × 17" (43 cm) wide.

Yarn
DK weight (#3 Light).

Shown here: Purl Soho Cotton Pure (100% pima cotton; 262 yd [240 m]/3½ oz[100 g]): #5740 Teacake Pink (MC), 3 hanks; #5680 Sea Pink (CC), 1 hank.

Needles
Size U.S. 6 (4 mm): 24" and 60" (60 and 152 cm) circular (cir).

Adjust needle size if necessary to obtain the correct gauge.

Notions
Markers (m); yarn needle.

Gauge
2 stitch pattern repeats (34 sts) = 5½" (14 cm) and 28 rows = 4" (10 cm) in Large Lace Chart.

Notes
⌐ Circular needles are recommended to accommodate the large number of stitches. Do not join; work back and forth in rows.

⌐ When picking up stitches along the selvedge for the border, the recommendation is to pick up one stitch between garter bumps, then pick up one stitch through the back of the next garter bump. Adjust pick-up rate as needed to spread stitches evenly along the length of the stole.

Stitch Guide

2×2 RIBBING (MULTIPLE OF 4 STS + 2)
Row 1: (WS) K1, p1, *k2, p2; rep from * to last 4 sts, k2, p1, k1.

Row 2: (RS) *K2, p2; rep from * to last 2 sts, k2.

Rep Rows 1 and 2 for patt.

body

Using MC and shorter cir needle, CO 86 sts. Do not join; work back and forth in rows.

Work in 2×2 Ribbing (see Stitch Guide) for 4 rows, ending after a RS row.

Next Row: (WS) Knit.

Inc Row: (RS) K21, [M1, k22] 2 times, M1, knit to end—89 sts.

Work Rows 1–36 of Lace Chart 11 times, then work Row 1 once more.

Dec Row: (RS) [K21, k2tog] 3 times, knit to end—86 sts rem.

Next Row: (WS) Knit.

Beg with a RS row, work 4 rows in 2×2 Ribbing, ending after a WS row.

BO all sts in patt.

BORDER

With CC and longer needles, and with RS facing, pick up and knit 306 sts along the length of the stole (about 3 sts for every 4 rows; see Notes). Do not join; work back and forth in rows.

Next Row: (WS) Knit.

Beg with a RS row, work 10 rows in 2×2 Ribbing. BO all sts in patt.

Rep for opposite side.

finishing

Weave in ends, wash and shape to measurements.

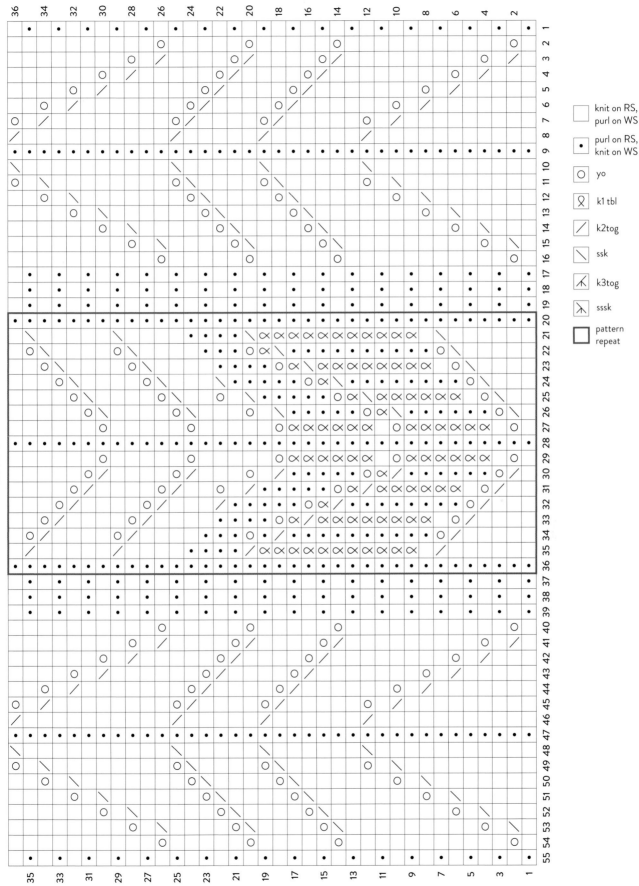

LACE CHART

knit on RS,
purl on WS

• purl on RS,
knit on WS

O yo

k1 tbl

/ k2tog

\ ssk

k3tog

sssk

pattern
repeat

nikko

tee

Greek; daylight

Summertime knits are always tricky—is the fiber itchy when it expands, imbued with humid air? Is it light enough, breezy enough, comfortable enough? This simple little pullover checks all the boxes. Not only is this everything I want in a warm-weather top, but it's a breeze to knit! There's nearly no shaping, simple stitches keep the knitting pleasant, and the color details elevate what could have been an ordinary piece.

Finished Sizes
33½ (36, 38½, 41, 43¾, 46¼, 48¾, 52, 54½)"
(85 [91.5, 98, 104, 111, 117.5, 124, 132, 138.5] cm) bust circumference.

Designed to fit 31 (33½, 36, 38½, 41¼, 43¾, 46¼, 49½, 52)" (78.5 [85, 91.5, 98, 105, 111, 117.5, 125.5, 132] cm) bust, with 2½" (6.5 cm) added for ease.

Sweater shown measures 38½" (98 cm) and fits a 36" (91.5 cm) bust.

Yarn
Fingering weight
(#1 Super Fine).

Shown here: Quince and Co. Sparrow (100% organic linen; 168 yd [155 m]/1¾ [50 g] hank): #251 Conch (MC), 4 (4, 5, 5, 6, 6, 7, 7, 8) hanks; #255 Mineral (CC), 1 (1, 1, 1, 1, 1, 2, 2, 2) hank(s).

Needles
Size U.S. 5 (3.75 mm): 24" (61 cm) circular (cir).

Adjust needle size if necessary to obtain the correct gauge.

Notions
Markers (m); extra needle for 3-needle Bind-off; yarn needle.

Gauge
25 sts and 28 rows/rnds = 4" (10 cm) in St st, blocked.

Notes
⌐ Worked from the bottom up in rounds, top front and back pieces are divided for the neck and armholes and are worked flat. Shoulder seams are joined using the 3-needle Bind-off method.

⌐ When working top pieces, colors can be carried up the side between color changes or broken, weaving in the ends in finishing.

Stitch Guide

1×1 RIBBING

Sizes 33½ (36, 38½, 41, 43¾, 46¼, 48¾)"
(85 [91.5, 98, 104, 111, 117.5, 124] cm) Only

Row 1: (RS) Sl1 pwise wyb, k2, *p1, k1; rep from * to last 3 sts, k3.

Row 2: Sl1 pwise wyf, k2, *p1, k1; rep from * to last 3 sts, k3.

Rep Rows 1 and 2 for patt.

Sizes 52 (54½)" (132 [138.5] cm) Only

Row 1: (RS) Sl1 pwise wyb, k2, *p1, k1; rep from * to last 4 sts, p1, k3.

Row 2: Sl1 pwise wyf, k2, *k1, p1; rep from * to last 4 sts, k4.

Rep Rows 1 and 2 for patt.

body

Using MC, CO 209 (225, 241, 257, 273, 289, 305, 325, 341) sts. Pm for beg of rnd, and join for working in the rnd, being careful not to twist sts.

Set-up Rnd: K52 (56, 60, 64, 68, 72, 76, 81, 85), pm for center front, sl1 pwise wyb, k52 (56, 60, 64, 68, 72, 76, 81, 85), pm for side, knit to end.

Rnd 1: K1, p2, knit to 3 sts before side m, p2, k1, slm, k1, p2, knit to last 3 sts, p2, k1.

Rnd 2: Knit to center front m, slm, sl1 pwise wyb, knit to end.

Rnd 3: (Garter Ridge) K1, purl to m, slm, k1, purl to one st before m, k1, slm, k1, purl to last st, k1.

Rep Rnds 1 and 2 until piece meas 12¾ (13, 13¼, 13½, 13½, 13½, 13¾, 13¾, 13¾)" (32.5 [33, 33.5, 34.5, 34.5, 34.5, 35, 35, 35] cm) from CO edge, ending after Rnd 1.

DIVIDE FRONT AND BACK

Next Rnd: Knit to center front m, remove m, BO 1, knit to side m, slm, knit across back. Do not break yarn. Turn and cont working back and forth in rows across Left Back sts only.

left back

Set-up Row: (WS) Sl1 pwise wyf, k51 (55, 59, 63, 67, 71, 75, 80, 84). Place rem 52 (56, 60, 64, 68, 72, 76, 81, 85) sts onto st holder or waste yarn for Right Back.

Rows 1 and 3: (RS) Sl1 pwise wyb, knit to end.

Rows 2 and 4: Sl1 pwise wyf, k2, purl to last 3 sts, k3.

Change to CC and work Rows 5 and 6 for your size as foll:

Sizes 33½ (36, 38½, 41, 43¾, 46¼, 48¾)"
(85 [91.5, 98, 104, 111, 117.5, 124] cm) Only
Row 5: (RS) Sl1 pwise wyb, k2, *(k1, yo, k1) into next st, sl1 pwise wyb; rep from * to last 3 sts, k3.

Row 6: Sl1 pwise wyf, k2, *sl1 pwise wyb, k3tog tbl; rep from * to last 3 sts, k3.

Sizes 52 (54½)" (132 [138.5] cm) Only
Row 5: (RS) Sl1 pwise wyb, k2, *(k1, yo, k1) into next st, sl1 pwise wyb; rep from * to last 4 sts, (k1, yo, k1) into next st, k3.

Row 6: Sl1 pwise wyf, k2, *k3tog tbl, sl1 pwise wyb; rep from * to last 6 sts, k3tog tbl, k3.

All Sizes
Break CC or carry up the side.

Rows 7, 9, and 11: Using MC, rep Row 1.

Rows 8 and 10: Rep Row 2.

Row 12: (WS) Sl1 pwise, knit to end.

Row 13: Rep Row 1.

Row 14: Rep Row 2.

Rows 15 and 17: Using CC, rep Row 1.

Rows 16 and 18: Rep Row 2. Break CC.

Rows 19 and 21: Using MC, rep Row 1.

Row 20: Rep Row 2.

Row 22: (WS) Sl1 pwise, knit to end.

Rep last 22 rows once more.

Sizes 48¾ (52, 54½)" (124 [132, 138.5] cm) Only
Rep Rows 1–6 once more.

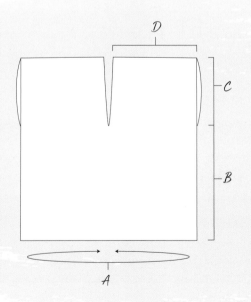

A: 33½ (36, 38½, 41, 43¾, 46¼, 48¾, 52, 54½)"
(85 [91.5, 98, 104, 111, 117.5, 124, 132, 138.5] cm)

B: 12¾ (13, 13¼, 13½, 13½, 13½, 13¾, 13¾, 13¾)"
(32.5 [33, 33.5, 34.5, 34.5, 34.5, 35, 35, 35] cm)

C: 7¼ (7¼, 7½, 7¾, 8, 8¼, 8½, 8½, 9)"
(18.5 [18.5, 19, 19.5, 20.5, 21, 21.5, 21.5, 23] cm)

D: 8¼ (9, 9½, 10¼, 11, 11½, 12¼, 13, 13½)"
(21 [23, 24, 26, 28, 29, 31, 33, 34.5] cm)

Cont in St st with MC only, working first and last 3 sts as est until armhole meas 6¼ (6¼, 6½, 6¾, 7, 7¼, 7½, 7½, 8)" (16 [16, 16.5, 17, 18, 18.5, 19, 19, 20.5] cm) from divide, ending after a WS row.

Work in 1×1 Ribbing for your size (see Stitch Guide) for 1" (2.5 cm), ending after a WS row.

Place Left Back sts onto st holder or waste yarn. Break yarn.

right back

Return 52 (56, 60, 64, 68, 72, 76, 81, 85) Right Back sts to needles and join MC with WS facing.

Set-up Row: (WS) Sl1 pwise wyf, knit to end.

Cont working as for Left Back.

left front

Work as for Right Back until armhole meas 6¼ (6¼, 6½, 6¾, 7, 7¼, 7½, 7½, 8)" (16 [16, 16.5, 17, 18, 18.5, 19, 19, 20.5] cm) from divide, ending after a WS row.

Work in 1×1 Ribbing for your size for 1¼" (3.2 cm), ending after a RS row.

Place Left Front sts onto st holder or waste yarn. Break yarn.

right front

Work as for Left Front until armhole meas 6¼ (6¼, 6½, 6¾, 7, 7¼, 7½, 7½, 8)" (16 [16, 16.5, 17, 18, 18.5, 19, 19, 20.5] cm) from divide, ending after a WS row.

Work in 1×1 Ribbing for your size for 1¼" (3.2 cm), ending after a RS row.

finishing

JOIN SHOULDERS

Return 52 (56, 60, 64, 68, 72, 76, 81, 85) Right Back sts to needles and hold them parallel to the Right Front sts. Beg at armhole edge, BO all sts using 3-needle BO (see Glossary), ending at the neck edge.

Rep for the left shoulder, beg at neck edge.

Weave in ends. Block to measurements.

quince
& CO.

Knitting summer garments is challenging enough as it is, isn't it? The unforgiving strands of fiber that are often too slippery or too stiff... the worry that once all that work's done, the garment won't get worn because it feels abrasive or heavy in those hot, humid months. This is a season I'm constantly challenging myself to design for, and Quince & Co. is one of those dependable companies with strong values that I know produces a product well-suited for the season it's designed for. Over the past few years, the company has found its way into the hearts of many knitters, but for those still unfamiliar with their products, there's a lot of information on their website about how Quince & Co. came to be, their dedication to local fibers, and their values as a company. Not only do they produce exceptional products, but their prices are well within most budgets.

I asked Quince & Co. to give us a peek behind the curtain. Pam Allen founded the company in 2010 in partnership with a historic mill in Maine. Beginning with a focus on wool yarns locally sourced and produced in the United States, Quince's offerings have since expanded to include natural fibers not readily available domestically. The organic linen in Sparrow and Kestrel is created from Belgian-grown flax spun in Italy.

To showcase the brand's many yarn options, Quince & Co. publishes knitting patterns, collections, and books. Upon Pam's retirement in 2017, her son Ryan Fitzgerald took ownership, with designer Leila Raabe stepping into the role of creative director. Quince's sister brands, Twig & Horn and Stone Wool Yarn, have since joined the flurry of creative activity and dedication to thoughtful production of goods for knitters and makers.

WHY SPARROW?

When I began whittling down my yarn selections, Sparrow kept finding itself at the top of the list because of the wide range of colors it comes in, but even more because of the addition of marled yarns in such a fine strand of linen. It's the attention to details like this that solidified my decision. Nikko is, at its core, the simplest shaped pullover you can create, but the yarn, both in the sophisticated and delicately saturated color and in the faint shine of the fiber, elevates the pullover.

dax

shell

French; water

This summer top has a bold silhouette accented by geometric color blocking. Worked from the bottom up in two pieces and using the simplest short-rows to create contrasting wedges, Dax takes you on an enjoyable knitting adventure. The side seams can be worked two ways, as outlined in the notes for the pattern.

Finished Sizes

40 (41½, 44¼, 48¾, 50¼, 53, 54½, 57½, 59)" (101.5 [105.5, 112.5, 124, 127.5, 134.5, 138.5, 146, 150] cm) bust circumference.

Designed to fit 31¾ (33¼, 36, 40½, 42, 44¾, 46¼, 49¼, 50¾)" (80.5 [84.5, 91.5, 103, 106.5, 113.5, 117.5, 125, 129] cm bust, with 8¼" (21 cm) added for ease.

Sweater shown measures 44¼" (112.5 cm) and fits a 36" (91.5 cm) bust.

Yarn

Fingering weight (#2 Fine).

Shown here: Berroco Remix Light (30% nylon, 27% cotton, 24% acrylic, 10% silk, 9% linen; 432 yd [400 m]/3½ oz [100 g]): #6901 Birch (MC), 2 (2, 2, 3, 3, 3, 3, 4, 4) balls; #6933 Patina (CC), 1 (1, 1, 2, 2, 2, 2, 3, 3) ball(s).

Needles

Size U.S. 5 (3.75 mm): set of 4 or 5 double-pointed (dpn) and 24" (60 cm) circular (cir).

Adjust needle size if necessary to obtain the correct gauge.

Notions

Markers (m); removable marker; stitch holders or waste yarn; yarn needle.

Gauge

22 sts and 38 rows = 4" (10 cm) in Garter st.

22 sts and 34 rows = 4" (10 cm) in St st worked flat.

Notes

⏜ The pattern instructs you to bind off the final row for the side panels so that the entire length of each side can be seamed, controlling the silhouette. However, for a seamless look, you can instead place these stitches onto waste yarn or spare needles and graft together using the Kitchener stitch (see Glossary).

⏜ Circular needle is recommended to accommodate large number of sts.

front

Using cir needle and MC, CO 110 (114, 122, 134, 138, 146, 150, 158, 162) sts. Do not join; work back and forth in rows.

Row 1: (WS) K1, p1, *k2, p2; rep from * to last 4 sts, k2, p1, k1.

Row 2: (RS) *K2, p2; rep from * to last 2 sts, k2.

Rep Rows 1 and 2 until piece meas 1¾" (4.5 cm) from CO, ending after a WS row. Break yarn.

Next Row: (RS) Place 42 (43, 46, 50, 52, 55, 56, 59, 61) sts onto st holder or waste yarn, rejoin yarn and k26 (28, 30, 34, 34, 36, 38, 40, 40), place rem 42 (43, 46, 50, 52, 55, 56, 59, 61) sts onto st holder or waste yarn, cont working back and forth over 26 (28, 30, 34, 34, 36, 38, 40, 40) center sts only.

SHAPE SIDES

Next Row: (WS) Sl1, knit to end.

Inc Row: (RS) Sl1, k1, M1L, knit to last 2 sts, M1R, k2—2 sts inc'd.

Rep last 2 rows 41 (42, 45, 49, 51, 54, 55, 58, 60) more times—110 (114, 122, 134, 138, 146, 150, 158, 162) sts.

Mark the last st of the last row with a removable marker as a guide for picking up sts later.

Cont working in Garter St (knit every row) until piece meas 12 (12½, 12¾, 12¾, 13¼, 14, 14¼, 14¾, 15¼)" (30.5 [32, 32.5, 32.5, 33.5, 35.5, 36, 37.5, 38.5] cm) from CO, ending after a WS row.

SHAPE ARMHOLES

BO 3 sts at the beg of the next 2 rows—104 (108, 116, 128, 132, 140, 144, 152, 156) sts rem.

Dec Row: (RS) Sl1, k2tog, knit to last 3 sts, ssk, k1—2 sts dec'd.

Next Row: Sl1, knit to end.

Rep last 2 rows 14 (15, 18, 23, 24, 26, 26, 29, 29) more times—74 (76, 78, 80, 82, 86, 90, 92, 96) sts rem.

Cont working in Garter st until armholes meas 5½ (5¾, 6, 6¼, 6¼, 6½, 6¾, 6¾, 7)" (14 [14.5, 15, 16, 16, 16.5, 17, 17, 18] cm) from underarm BO sts, ending after a WS row.

SHAPE NECKLINE

Next Row: (RS) Sl1, k27 (28, 28, 28, 28, 29, 30, 29, 30) for Left Front, place next 18 (18, 20, 22, 24, 26, 28, 32, 34) sts onto st holder or waste yarn for neck, place rem 28 (29, 29, 29, 29, 30, 31, 30, 31) sts onto st holder or waste yarn for Right Front. Cont working over Left Front sts only.

Left Front

Next Row: (WS) Sl1, knit to end.

Dec Row: Sl1, knit to last 3 sts, ssk, k1—1 st dec'd.

Rep last 2 rows 5 more times—22 (23, 23, 23, 23, 24, 25, 24, 25) sts rem.

Next Row: (WS) Sl1, knit to end.

SHAPE LEFT FRONT SHOULDER

Next Row: (RS) BO 3 sts, knit to end—19 (20, 20, 20, 20, 21, 22, 21, 22) sts rem.

Next Row: Sl1, knit to end.

Rep last 2 rows 2 more times—13 (14, 14, 14, 14, 15, 16, 15, 16) sts rem.

BO all sts knitwise. Break yarn.

Right Front

Return 28 (29, 29, 29, 29, 30, 31, 30, 31) held Right Front sts to needle and rejoin MC at neck edge.

Next Row: (RS) Sl1, knit to end.

Next Row: (WS) Sl1, knit to end.

Dec Row: Sl1, k2tog, knit to end—1 st dec'd.

Rep last 2 rows 5 more times—22 (23, 23, 23, 23, 24, 25, 24, 25) sts rem.

SHAPE RIGHT FRONT SHOULDER

Next Row: (WS) BO 3 sts, knit to end—19 (20, 20, 20, 20, 21, 22, 21, 22) sts rem.

Next Row: Sl1, knit to end.

Rep last 2 rows 2 more times—13 (14, 14, 14, 14, 15, 16, 15, 16) sts rem.

BO all sts. Break yarn.

FRONT LEFT SIDE PANEL

Return 42 (43, 46, 50, 52, 55, 56, 59, 61) held sts from left front hem to needle. With RS facing, join CC and knit across, rotate work counterclockwise, pick up and knit 42 (43, 46, 50, 52, 55, 56, 59, 61) sts along slip-st edge of Front—84 (86, 92, 100, 104, 110, 112, 118, 122) sts.

Short-row 1: (WS) Sl1, p42 (43, 46, 50, 52, 55, 56, 59, 61), turn.

Short-row 2: Sl1, k1, turn—41 (42, 45, 49, 51, 54, 55, 58, 60) sts rem unworked on each end of row.

Short-row 3: Sl1, purl to 1 st before gap, close gap (see Glossary), p1, turn.

Short-row 4: Sl1, knit to 1 st before gap, close gap, k1, turn.

Rep last 2 short-rows 39 (40, 43, 47, 49, 52, 54, 56, 58) more times—1 st rem unworked on each side.

Next Row: (WS) Sl1, purl to 1 st before gap, close gap, purl to end.

BO all sts, closing rem gap. Break yarn.

FRONT RIGHT SIDE PANEL

With RS facing, using CC and longer needles, beg near right armhole, pick up and knit 42 (43, 46, 50, 52, 55, 56, 59, 61) sts along slip-st edge of Front, rotate work counterclockwise, return 42 (43, 46, 50, 52, 55, 56, 59, 61) held sts from right front hem to empty end of needle and knit across—84 (86, 92, 100, 104, 110, 112, 118, 122) sts.

Work short-rows as for Front Left Side Panel.

back

Work as for Front until armhole meas 5½ (5¾, 6, 6¼, 6¼, 6½, 6¾, 6¾, 7)" (14 [14.5, 15, 16, 16, 16.5, 17, 17, 18] cm) from underarm BO sts, ending after a WS row—74 (76, 78, 80, 82, 86, 90, 92, 96) sts.

SHAPE NECKLINE

Next Row: (RS) Sl1, k27 (28, 28, 28, 28, 29, 30, 29, 30), pm, k18 (18, 20, 22, 24, 26, 28, 32, 34), pm, 28 (29, 29, 29, 29, 30, 31, 30, 31).

Next Row: (WS) Sl1, knit to end.

Dec Row: (RS) Sl1, knit to 3 sts before m, k2tog, k1, slm, knit to m, slm, k1, ssk, knit to end—2 sts dec'd.

Rep last 2 rows 5 more times—62 (64, 66, 68, 70, 74, 78, 80, 84) sts rem.

Next Row: (WS) Sl1, knit to end.

LEFT BACK
Shape Left Back Shoulder

Row 1: (RS) BO 3 sts, knit to m, place next 18 (18, 20, 22, 24, 26, 28, 32, 34) sts onto st holder or waste yarn for neck, place rem 22 (23, 23, 23, 23, 24, 25, 24, 25) sts onto separate st holder or waste yarn for Right Back—19 (20, 20, 20, 20, 21, 22, 21, 22) sts rem.

Row 2: Sl1, knit to end.

Row 3: BO 3 sts, knit to end—16 (17, 17, 17, 17, 18, 19, 18, 19) sts rem.

Rows 4–6: Rep Rows 2 and 3 once, then rep Row 2 one more time—13 (14, 14, 14, 14, 15, 16, 15, 16) sts rem.

BO all sts and break yarn.

RIGHT BACK
Return 22 (23, 23, 23, 23, 24, 25, 24, 25) held Right Back sts to needle and join MC to RS.

Shape Right Back Shoulder
Row 1: (RS) Sl1, knit to end.

Row 2: BO 3, knit to end—19 (20, 20, 20, 20, 21, 22, 21, 22) sts rem.

Rows 3–7: Rep Rows 1 and 2 twice, then rep Row 1 one more time—13 (14, 14, 14, 14, 15, 16, 15, 16) sts rem.

BO all sts and break yarn.

BACK RIGHT SIDE PANEL
Work as Front Right Side Panel.

BACK LEFT SIDE PANEL
Work as Front Left Side Panel.

finishing

Seam Front and Back Shoulders.

Seam sides, leaving the ribbed hem unworked for a split hemline, or seam only the main color at the underarm and graft the contrasting color as described in Notes.

Weave in ends and block to measurements.

With dpns and RS facing, beg at left shoulder seam, pick up and knit 11 sts along front left neckline, place 18 (18, 20, 22, 24, 26, 28, 32, 34) held Front sts onto empty needle and knit across, pick up and knit 11 sts along front right neckline, pick up and knit 4 sts along back right neckline, place 18 (18, 20, 22, 24, 26, 28, 32, 34) held Back sts onto empty needle and knit across, pick up and knit 4 sts along back left neckline, pm, and join for working in the rnd—66 (66, 70, 74, 78, 82, 86, 94, 98) sts.

Purl 1 rnd.

BO all sts using Elastic Bind-off (see Glossary).

Weave in rem ends.

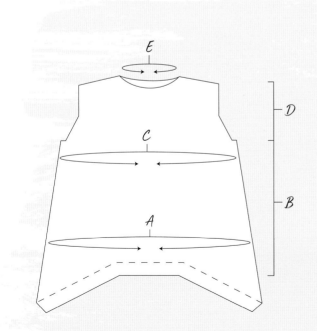

A: 48 (49¾, 53¼, 58½, 60¼, 64, 65½, 69¼, 71)"
122 (126.5, 135, 148.5, 153, 162.5, 166.5, 176, 180.5) cm)

B: 12 (12½, 12¾, 12¾, 13¼, 14, 14¼, 14¾, 15¼)"
30.5 [32, 32.5, 32.5, 33.5, 35.5, 36, 37.5, 38.5] cm)

C: 40 (41½, 44¼, 48¾, 50¼, 53, 54½, 57½, 59)"
101.5 [105.5, 112.5, 124, 127.5, 134.5, 138.5, 146, 150] cm)

D: 7 (7¼, 7½, 7¾, 7¾, 8, 8¼, 8¼, 8½)"
18 [18.5, 19, 19.5, 19.5, 20.5, 21, 21, 21.5] cm)

E: 12 (12, 12¾, 13½, 14¼, 15, 15¾, 17, 17¾)"
30.5 [30.5, 32.5, 34.5, 36, 38, 40, 43, 45] cm)

isla
vest

Scottish; island

This vest-style cardigan with clean lines is designed to be worn open or with an I-cord tie. The lightweight linen, perfect for sticky summer weather, is accented with simple colorwork at the shoulders. Beginner-level stitches and straightforward shaping make this a great piece for knitters with a variety of skill sets—and the duplicate stitch provides an opportunity to learn a very easy technique that packs a visual punch.

Finished Sizes
33¼ (35¼, 38, 40, 43¼, 45¼, 48, 50¾, 53¼)" (84.5 [89.5, 96.5, 101.5, 110, 115, 122, 129, 135] cm) bust circumference.

Designed to fit 33¼ (35¼, 38, 40, 43¼, 45¼, 48, 50¾, 53¼)" (84.5 [89.5, 96.5, 101.5, 110, 115, 122, 129, 135] cm) bust with no ease.

Vest shown measures 35¼" (89.5 cm) and fits a 35¼" (89.5 cm) bust.

Yarn
DK weight (#3 Light).

Shown here: Fibra Natura Flax (100% linen; 137 yd [125 m]/1¾ oz [50 g]): #16 Taupe (MC), 6 (7, 8, 8, 9, 9, 10, 11, 12) hanks; #15 Black (CC), 1 hank.

Needles
Hem and I-cord: Size U.S. 4 (3.5 mm): 32" (80 cm) circular (cir) and set of 4 or 5 double-pointed (dpn).

Body: Size U.S. 6 (4 mm): 32" (80 cm) cir.

Adjust needle size if necessary to obtain the correct gauge.

Notions
Markers (m); stitch holders or waste yarn; yarn needle.

Gauge
24 sts and 26 rows = 4" (10 cm) in St st on larger needles.

Notes
⟶ Worked flat from the bottom up, this cardigan is worked in one piece with only two seams.

⟶ Circular needle is recommended to accommodate large number of sts.

⟶ When working duplicate stitch, make sure the blocked fabric is completely dry; it may be useful to work with the piece on a hanger, which encourages even tension.

hem

Using smaller cir needles and MC, CO 234 (250, 270, 290, 302, 322, 342, 358, 378) sts. Do not join; work back and forth in rows.

EST 2×2 RIBBING

Row 1: (WS) K1, p1, *k2, p2; rep from * to last 4 sts, k2, p1, k1.

Row 2: (RS) *K2, p2; rep from * to last 2 sts, k2.

Rep Rows 1 and 2 until piece meas 2¼" (5.5 cm) from CO edge, ending after a WS row.

Eyelet Row: (RS) K2, p1, *K2tog, yo twice, ssk; rep from * to last 3 sts, p1, k2.

Next Row: K1, p1, k1, *p1, purl into first yo, knit into second yo, p1; rep from * to last 3 sts, k1, p1, k1.

body

Change to larger needles.

EST ST ST

Row 1: (RS) K2, p1, knit to last 3 sts, p1, k2.

Row 2: (WS) K1, p1, k1, purl to last 3 sts, k1, p1, k1.

Rep Rows 1 and 2 until piece meas 8½" (21.5 cm) from CO edge, ending on a RS row.

SHAPE WAIST

Set-up Row: (WS) Work in patt for 58 (62, 67, 73, 75, 80, 85, 89, 94) sts, pm, p118 (126, 136, 144, 152, 162, 172, 180, 190), pm, work in patt for 58 (62, 67, 73, 75, 80, 85, 89, 94) sts to end.

Dec Row: (RS) *Work in patt as est to 4 sts before m, k2tog, k2, sl m, k2, ssk; rep from * once more, work in patt as est to end—4 sts dec'd.

Next Row: K1, p1, k1, purl to last 3 sts, k1, p1, k1.

Rep last 2 rows 8 (9, 10, 11, 10, 12, 13, 13, 14) more times—198 (210, 226, 242, 258, 270, 286, 302, 318) sts rem.

Work even in patt as est without decreasing further until piece meas 18 (18¼, 18½, 18½, 18½, 18½, 18½, 18½, 18½)" (45.5 [46.5, 47, 47, 47, 47, 47, 47, 47] cm) from CO edge, ending after a WS row.

DIVIDE BACK AND FRONTS

Next Row: (RS) K2, p1, knit to 3 sts before m, p1, k2, remove m, place next 100 (106, 114, 120, 130, 136, 144, 152, 160) sts onto st holder or waste yarn for back, then place the rem 49 (52, 56, 61, 64, 67, 71, 75, 79) sts onto a separate st holder or waste yarn for Left Front. Cont working 49 (52, 56, 61, 64, 67, 71, 75, 79) Right Front sts.

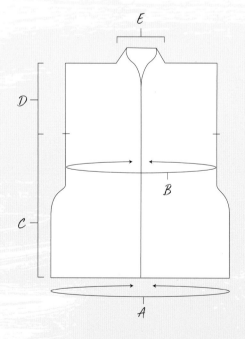

A: 39 (41¾, 45, 48¼, 50¼, 53¾, 57, 59¾, 63)"
99 [106, 114.5, 122.5, 127.5, 136.5, 145, 152, 160] cm)

B: 33¼ (35¼, 38, 40, 43¼, 45¼, 48, 50¾, 53¼)"
84.5 [89.5, 96.5, 101.5, 110, 115, 122, 129, 135] cm)

C: 18 (18¼, 18½, 18½, 18½, 18½, 18½, 18½, 18½)"
45.5 [46.5, 47, 47, 47, 47, 47, 47, 47] cm)

D: 8 (8¼, 8½, 8¾, 9, 9¼, 9¼, 9¾, 9¾)"
20.5 [21, 21.5, 22, 23, 23.5, 23.5, 25, 25] cm)

E: 6¼ (7, 7¾, 7¼, 7¾, 7¾, 8¼, 8¼, 9)"
16 [18, 19.5, 18.5, 19.5, 19.5, 21, 21, 23] cm)

right front

Row 1: (WS) K1, p1, k1, purl to last 3 sts, k1, p1, k1.

Row 2: (RS) K2, p1, knit to last 3 sts, p1, k2.

Work even in patt as est until armhole meas 4¼ (4½, 4¾, 5, 5¼, 5½, 5½, 6, 6)" (11 [11.5, 12, 12.5, 13.5, 14, 14, 15, 15] cm), ending after a WS row.

Change to CC and work 2 rows in patt as est.

Change to MC and work 2 rows in patt as est.

Change to CC and work 2 rows in patt as est.

Break CC.

Using MC, work even in patt as est for 17 rows, ending after a RS row.

Next Row: (WS) Work in patt as est over first 31 (32, 34, 38, 42, 45, 47, 51, 53) sts for shoulder, pm, work in patt as est over last 18 (20, 22, 23, 22, 22, 24, 24, 26) sts for neckband.

Break yarn and place sts onto st holder or waste yarn.

back

Return 100 (106, 114, 120, 130, 136, 144, 152, 160) held Back sts to larger needle and rejoin MC with RS facing.

EST ST ST

Row 1: (RS) K2, p1, knit to last 3 sts, p1, k2.

Row 2: K1, p1, k1, purl to last 3 sts, k1, p1, k1.

Work even in patt as est until armhole meas 8 (8¼, 8½, 8¾, 9, 9¼, 9¼, 9¾, 9¾)" (20.5 [21, 21.5, 22, 23, 23.5, 23.5, 25, 25] cm), ending after a RS row.

DIVIDE FOR NECK

Next Row: (WS) Work in patt as est over first 31 (32, 34, 38, 42, 45, 47, 51, 53) sts, pm, p19 (21, 23, 22, 23, 23, 25, 25, 27), place contrasting marker for center of Back neck, p19 (21, 23, 22, 23, 23, 25, 25, 27), pm, work in patt as est over last 31 (32, 34, 38, 42, 45, 47, 51, 53) sts.

Break yarn and place sts onto st holder or waste yarn.

left front

Return 49 (52, 56, 61, 64, 67, 71, 75, 79) held Left Front sts to larger needle and rejoin MC with RS facing.

Next Row: (RS) K2, p1, knit to last 3 sts, p1, k2.

Work as for Right Front until the marker is placed between the shoulder and neckband.

Next Row: (WS) Work in patt as est over first 18 (20, 22, 23, 22, 22, 24, 24, 26) sts for neckband, pm, work in patt as est over last 31 (32, 34, 38, 42, 45, 47, 51, 53) sts for shoulder.

Break yarn.

finishing

JOIN LEFT SHOULDER
Return 31 (32, 34, 38, 42, 45, 47, 51, 53) Left Back shoulder sts to larger needles. With RS of Front facing and beg at the armhole, graft Left Front and Back shoulder together using Kitchener st (see Glossary).

JOIN RIGHT SHOULDER
Return 31 (32, 34, 38, 42, 45, 47, 51, 53) Right Back and Right Front shoulder sts to larger needles. With RS of Back facing and beg at the armhole, graft Right Front and Back shoulder together using Kitchener st.

RIGHT NECKBAND
Return 18 (20, 22, 23, 22, 22, 24, 24, 26) held Right Front neckband sts and 19 (21, 23, 22, 23, 23, 25, 25, 27) held Right Back neck sts to larger needle and join yarn with RS facing—37 (41, 45, 45, 45, 45, 49, 49, 53) sts.

Dec Row: (RS) K2, p1, k14 (15, 18, 19, 18, 18, 20, 20, 22), sl1, k1 from Back neck, psso, turn—1 st dec'd.

Next Row: Sl1 pwise, purl to last 3 sts, k1, p1, k1.

Rep last 2 rows 19 (20, 22, 21, 22, 22, 24, 24, 26) more times—18 (20, 22, 23, 22, 22, 24, 24, 26) sts rem.

Place Right Neckband sts onto st holder or waste yarn. Break yarn.

LEFT NECKBAND
Return 18 (20, 22, 23, 22, 22, 24, 24, 26) held Left Front neckband sts to larger needle and join yarn with RS facing.

DUPLICATE STITCH CHART

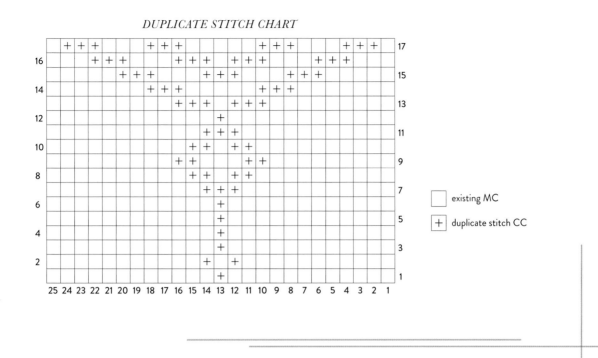

existing MC

+ duplicate stitch CC

Set-up Row: (RS) Knit to last 3 sts, p1, k2.

Place 19 (21, 23, 22, 23, 23, 25, 25, 27) held Left Back neck sts onto needle with the neckband sts—37 (41, 45, 45, 45, 45, 49, 49, 53) sts.

Dec Row: (WS) K1, p1, k1, k14 (15, 18, 19, 18, 18, 20, 20, 22), sl1, p1 from Back Neck, psso, turn.

Next Row: Sl1 pwise, knit to last 3 sts, p1, k2.

Rep last 2 rows 19 (20, 22, 21, 22, 22, 24, 24, 26) more times—18 (20, 22, 23, 22, 22, 24, 24, 26) sts rem.

Join Neckbands

Return 18 (20, 22, 23, 22, 22, 24, 24, 26) held Right Neckband sts to larger needle. Holding Right and Left Neckband needles parallel, with WS together, join using 3-needle BO (see Glossary), starting at the edge of the neckband and working toward the sweater neckline.

Wash sweater well in cool water, lay flat, shape to measurements, and let dry.

I-CORD LOOPS (MAKE 2)

Using MC, create a loop measuring about 1" (2.5 cm) and secure to the RS of the fabric about 5 (5¼, 5½, 5½, 5½, 5½, 5½, 5½, 5½)" (12.5 [13.5, 14, 14, 14, 14, 14, 14, 14] cm) down from the underarm to hold the I-cord tie.

Rep for the opposite side.

I-CORD TIE

Work I-cord tie using an I-cord machine or as foll:

Using dpns and MC, CO 4 sts. *Slide sts to opposite side of the dpn, k4; rep from * until tie meas 57 (60, 63, 66, 69, 72, 75, 78, 81)" (145 [152.5, 160, 167.5, 175.5, 183, 190.5, 198, 205.5] cm).

Weave in ends and knot each end of the tie.

SHOULDER DETAILS

Using about 40" (101.5 cm) of CC and a yarn needle, work duplicate stitch (see Glossary) patt from Duplicate Stitch Chart on each shoulder as foll:

Starting on the first MC row after the CC stripes at the shoulder, count over 24 (25, 27, 29, 31, 33, 35, 37, 39) sts from the armhole opening edge. This is the placement of the first st, located at row 1, column 13 of the chart. Follow the chart, placing the duplicate sts as indicated.

Weave in rem ends and steam-block duplicate stitch.

idalia
tank

Germanic; behold the sun

This summery top is cropped to fall just below the waistline, worked from the bottom up and featuring 2-color brioche for the body. Linen is the perfect fiber to add drape and air flow to Idalia, but the recommended yarn is far from the stiff linens we often think of, best reserved for housewares; it's perfectly smooth against the skin for wearables

Finished Sizes
34 (37¼, 40¾, 44, 46¾, 50, 53¼, 56¾)" (86.5 [94.5, 103.5, 112, 118.5, 127, 135.5, 144] cm) bust circumference.

Designed to fit 28 (31¼, 32¾, 36, 38¾, 42, 45¼, 48¾)" (71 [79.5, 83, 91.5, 98.5, 106.5, 115, 124] cm) bust, with 6–8" (15-20.5 cm) added for ease.

Sweater shown measures 44" (112 cm) and fits a 36" (91.5 cm) bust.

Yarn
Fingering weight (#1 Superfine).

Shown here: Shibui Reed (100% linen; 246 yd [225 m]/1¾ oz [50 g]): #13 Caffeine (MC), 2 (2, 2, 2, 3, 3, 3, 3) hanks; #2032 Field (CC), 1 (2, 2, 2, 2, 2, 3, 3) hank(s).

Needles
Body: Size U.S. 6 (4 mm): 24" or 32" (60 or 80 cm) circular (cir).

Neckband: Size U.S. 5 (3.75 mm): 16" (40 cm) cir.

Adjust needle size if necessary to obtain the correct gauge.

Notions
Markers (m); stitch holders or waste yarn; yarn needle.

Gauge
24 sts and 22 rnds = 4" (10 cm) in 2-color Brioche, blocked. Round count is only MC sts measured on RS of fabric.

Notes
↪ Tension can be tricky when working the brioche stitch in plant fibers, but it's more important to be consistent than it is to keep everything tight and tidy. Focus on keeping the same tension throughout your work, only tightening up edges as needed. Once finished, wash, shape, and dry the fabric flat; this causes the stitches to even out.

Stitch Guide

TWISTED RIB (MULTIPLE OF 2 STS)
Rnd 1: *K1 tbl, p1; rep from * to end.

Rep Rnd 1 for patt.

2-COLOR BRIOCHE
Worked in rounds (multiple of 2 sts)
Rnd 1: Using MC, *k1, sl1yo; rep from * to end.

Rnd 2: Join CC, *sl1yo, brp; rep from * to end

Rnd 3: Using MC, *brk, sl1yo; rep from * to end.

Rnd 4: Using CC, *sl1yo, brp; rep from * to end.

Rep Rnds 3 and 4 for patt.

BRLSL DEC
Slip the first stitch kwise, brk the following two stitches together (*fig. 1*), pass the slipped stitch over (*fig. 2*)—1 st decreased.

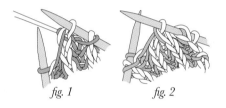

fig. 1   *fig. 2*

BRRSL DEC
Slip the first stitch (and its yo) kwise (*fig. 1*), knit the next stitch, pass the slipped stitch over (*fig. 2*), place stitch onto left-hand needle and pass the following stitch over, place st onto right-hand needle (*fig. 3*)—1 st decreased.

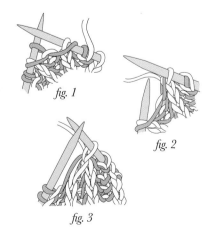

fig. 1

fig. 2

fig. 3

body

Using MC, CO 204 (224, 244, 264, 280, 300, 320, 340) sts. Pm for beg of rnd and join for working in the rnd, being careful not to twist sts.

Work Twisted Rib (see Stitch Guide) until piece meas 1 (1, 1, 1, 1¼, 1¼, 1½, 1½)" 2.5 [2.5, 2.5, 2.5, 3.2, 3.2, 3.8, 3.8] cm) from CO edge.

Work in 2-color Brioche patt (see Stitch Guide) until piece meas 7¾ (8, 8¼, 8¼, 8½, 8½, 8¾, 8¾)" (19.5 [20.5, 21, 21, 21.5, 21.5, 22, 22] cm) from CO edge, ending after Rnd 4 of patt.

EST UNDERARM PATT
Set-up Rnd: Using MC, *brk, k1, brk, pm, [sl1yo, brk] 49 (54, 59, 64, 68, 73, 78, 83) times, sl1yo, pm for side; rep from * once more.

Rnd 1: Using CC, *p3, slm, [brp, sl1yo] to 1 st before m, brp, slm; rep from * once more.

Rnd 2: Using MC, *k3, slm, [sl1yo, brk] to 1 st before m, sl1yo, slm, k3; rep from * once more.

Rep last 2 rnds until piece meas 8¾ (9, 9¼, 9¼, 9½, 9½, 9¾, 9¾)" (22 [23, 23.5, 23.5, 24, 24, 25, 25] cm) from CO edge, ending after a CC Rnd 1.

Dec Rnd: Using MC, *k2tog, k1, slm, [sl1yo, brk] to 1 st before m, sl1yo, slm; rep from * once more—2 sts dec'd; 202 (222, 242, 262, 278, 298, 318, 338) sts rem.

DIVIDE FRONT AND BACK
Next Rnd: Using CC, sl1 pwise wyb, p1, remove m, [brp, sl1yo] to 1 st before m, brp, remove m, p1, place next 101 (111, 121, 131, 139, 149, 159, 169) sts onto st holder or waste yarn for Back. Cont working in rows over 101 (111, 121, 131, 139, 149, 159, 169) Front sts only.

front

Do not turn work, slide sts to other end of needle to start a RS row.

Set-up Row: (RS) Using MC, k1, [sl1yo, brk] to last 2 sts, sl1yo, k1, turn.

Row 1A: (WS) Using CC, k1, [brk, sl1yo] to last 2 sts, brk, k1.

Slide sts to start another WS row.

Row 2A: Using MC, p1, [sl1yo, brp] to last 2 sts, sl1yo, p1, turn.

Row 1B: (RS) Using CC, p1, [brp, sl1yo] to last 2 sts, brp, p1.

Slide sts to start another RS row.

Row 2B, Dec Row: Using MC, k1, sl1yo, brk, sl1yo, brLsl dec (see Stitch Guide), [sl1yo, brk] to last 8 sts, sl1yo, brRsl dec (see Stitch Guide), sl1yo, brk, sl1yo, k1—4 sts dec'd.

Rep Rows 1A–2B of 2-color Brioche patt 10 (11, 12, 13, 13, 15, 15, 16) more times—57 (63, 69, 75, 83, 85, 95, 101) sts rem.

Rep Rows 1A–1B once more.

BIND OFF FRONT NECK AS FOLL:

Next Row: (RS) Using MC, k1, [sl1yo, brk] 5 times, sl1yo, BO 33 (39, 45, 51, 59, 61, 71, 77), work in patt as est to end—12 sts rem on each side.

Break yarn. Place all sts onto st holders or waste yarn.

back

Return 101 (111, 121, 131, 139, 149, 159, 169) held Back sts to larger needle and join CC with RS facing.

Set-up Row: (RS) Using CC, p1, [brp, sl1yo] to last 2 sts, brp, p1.

Slide sts to start another RS row and work same as Front, beg with Set-up Row—12 sts rem on each side when Back is complete.

Do not break yarn. Keep sts on needle.

neckband

Next Row: (RS) Using smaller needles and MC, [p1, brk] to end of Right Back sts, use the Backward Loop method (see Glossary) to CO 14 (18, 22, 26, 30, 34, 38, 42) sts, [p1, brk] to end of Left Back sts, CO 6 sts, [p1, brk] to end of Left Front sts, CO 10 (14, 16, 20, 24, 28, 32, 36) sts, [p1, brk] to end of Right Front sts, CO 3, pm for beg of rnd, CO 3 sts—84 (92, 98, 106, 114, 122, 130, 138) sts.

Next Rnd: *P1, k1 tbl; rep from * to end.

Rep last rnd 7 more times.

BO loosely in patt.

finishing

Weave in ends. Wash in cold water, shape, and dry flat.

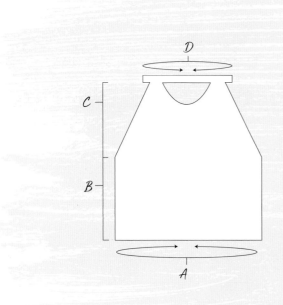

A: 34 (37¼, 40¾, 44, 46¾, 50, 53¼, 56¾)"
(86.5 [94.5, 103.5, 112, 118.5, 127, 135.5, 144] cm)

B: 8¾ (9, 9¼, 9¼, 9½, 9½, 9¾, 9¾)"
(22 [23, 23.5, 23.5, 24, 24, 25, 25] cm)

C: 4½ (4¾, 5¼, 5½, 5½, 6¼, 6¼, 6¾)"
(11.5 [12, 13.5, 14, 14, 16, 16, 17] cm)

D: 14 (15¼, 16¼, 17¾, 19, 20¼, 21¾, 23)"
(35.5 [38.5, 41.5, 45, 48.5, 51.5, 55, 58.5] cm)

Blown from the west,
Fallen leaves gather
In the east.

— YOSA BUSON

chapter four

Autumn

TEXTURES

Probably the universal knitting season, autumn brings images of fire crackling, woolly sweaters, and seeing your breath in the chilled air. There's a specific light and an atmosphere that goes beyond pumpkin spice. It's the smell of fallen leaves and wet earth, the sound of nature's slowing pace. Lots of texture and cable accents in slightly heavier yarns are called for here, with woolly pieces for the eventual transition into heavier layers, each piece having generous ease for a casual fit.

qui
mock-turtle

Chinese; autumn

*Simple construction and the easiest of stitches combine to make
a casual sweater for everyday wear. This is a great introduction
to side-to-side sweater construction that's relaxing to knit with
but a small amount of seaming to finish. The high collar is chic
and cozy, perfect for those chilly autumn days.*

Finished Size

33 (38, 42, 46, 50, 53,
58)" (84 [96.5, 106.5, 117,
127, 134.5, 147.5] cm) bust
circumference.

Designed to fit 32 (36, 40,
44, 48, 52, 56)" (81.5 [91.5,
101.5, 112, 122, 132, 142] cm)
bust, with 1–2" (2.5–5 cm)
added for ease.

Sweater shown measures
38" (96.5 cm) and fits a
36" (91.5 cm) bust.

Yarn

DK weight (#3 Light).

Shown here: YOTH Yarns
Big Sister (80% Merino
wool, 10% cashmere, 10%
nylon; 231 yd [211 m]/3½ oz
[100 g]): Ginger Root, 6 (6,
7, 7, 8, 8, 9) hanks.

Needles

Size U.S. 7 (4.5 mm):
32" (80 cm) circular (cir).

Size U.S. 7 (4.5 mm) crochet
hook for provisional cast-on.

*Adjust needle size if necessary
to obtain the correct gauge.*

Notions

Markers (m); removable
marker; stitch holders; waste
yarn; yarn needle.

Gauge

18 sts and 32 rows =
4" (10 cm) in Garter Ridge
St worked flat.

Notes

⌐ Worked from side to side,
starting and ending at the
sleeve cuffs, this pullover is
worked flat in one piece with
minimal finishing.

⌐ Circular needle is recommended to accommodate
large number of sts. Do not
join; work back and forth in
rows.

BROKEN SEED STITCH

(multiple of 2 sts + 1)

Row 1: (RS) *K1, p1; rep from * to last st, k1.

Row 2: (WS) K1, purl to last st, k1.

Row 3: Knit.

Row 4: Rep Row 2.

Rep Rows 1–4 for patt.

GARTER RIDGE STITCH

Row 1: (RS) Purl.

Row 2: (WS) Purl.

Row 3: Knit.

Row 4: Purl.

Rep Rows 1–4 for patt.

left sleeve

Using longer needle, CO 37 (43, 45, 45, 47, 47, 49) sts. Do not join; work back and forth in rows.

EST CUFF PATT

Next Row: (WS) Knit.

Inc Row: (RS) K1, M1L, knit to last st, M1R, k1—39 (45, 47, 47, 49, 49, 51) sts.

Next Row: K1, purl to last st, k1.

Work 4 (4, 4, 3, 3, 3, 2) rows in Broken Seed St (see Stitch Guide).

SHAPE SLEEVE

Inc Row: K1, M1L on knit rows or M1P on purl rows, work in patt as est to last st, M1R on knit rows or M1P on purl rows, k1—2 sts inc'd.

Work 5 (5, 5, 4, 4, 4, 3) rows even in patt as est.

Rep the last 6 (6, 6, 5, 5, 5, 4) rows 5 (5, 5, 7, 7, 7, 9) more times—51 (57, 59, 63, 65, 65, 71) sts.

Next Row: Rep Inc Row—53 (59, 61, 65, 67, 67, 73) sts.

Work 3 (3, 3, 0, 0, 0, 1) row(s) even, ending after Row 4 of Broken Seed St.

EST GARTER RIDGE

Cont shaping sleeve and est Garter Ridge St as foll:

Next Row: (RS) K1, work Garter Ridge St (see Stitch Guide) to last st, k1.

Work 1 (1, 1, 3, 3, 3, 1) row(s) in Garter Ridge St as est, maintaining the first and last sts in Garter St.

Next Row: Rep Inc Row—2 sts inc'd.

Work 5 (5, 5, 4, 4, 4, 3) rows even in patt as est.

Rep the last 6 (6, 6, 5, 5, 5, 4) rows 12 (11, 12, 12, 13, 15, 14) more times—79 (83, 87, 91, 95, 99, 103) sts.

Cont working 0 (6, 0, 11, 6, 0, 22) rows even in Garter Ridge St as est, until Rows 1–4 of patt have been completed a total of 20 (20, 20, 20, 20, 21, 21) times.

Next Row: (RS) K1, work Row 1 of Garter Ridge St to last st, k1.

Next Row: K1, p38 (40, 42, 44, 46, 48, 50), place a removable marker into the next st to mark the center, purl to last st, k1. Break yarn.

left body

CAST ON FOR BODY

Next Row: (RS) Hold work as if to begin working a RS row, CO 68 (71, 73, 73, 73, 73, 73) sts onto the RH needle for side seam, then use the same needle to work the following sts: k10, pm, knit to center st, M1R, k1, M1L, knit to end, turn, CO 68 (71, 73, 73, 73, 73, 73) sts for side seam—217 (227, 235, 239, 243, 247, 251) sts.

SHAPE LEFT SHOULDER

Row 1: (WS) K10, pm, purl to m, k10.

Rows 2 and 3: Knit to m, slm, purl to m, slm, knit to end.

Row 4, Inc Row: (RS) Knit to center st, M1R, k1, M1L, knit to end—2 sts inc'd.

Rep last 4 rows 2 more times—223 (233, 241, 245, 249, 253, 257) sts.

Next Row: (WS) K10, slm, work Row 4 of Garter Ridge St to last 10 sts, slm, k10.

Work even in Garter Ridge St and knitting the first and last 10 sts of each row, until piece meas 5½ (6, 7, 8, 9, 9½, 10½)" (14 [15, 18, 20.5, 23, 24, 26.5] cm) from body CO and ending after RS Row 1 of patt.

back

Next Row: (WS) Knit to m, slm, purl front sts to center st, BO center st removing m, purl back sts to m, slm, knit to end—111 (116, 120, 122, 124, 126, 128) sts each Front and Back.

Cont working Back sts only, place Front sts onto waste yarn.

LEFT NECK SHAPING

Row 1, Dec Row: (RS) Knit to m, slm, work Row 3 of Garter Ridge St to last 3 sts, k2tog, k1—1 st dec'd.

Row 2: (WS) K1, work Row 4 of Garter Ridge St to m, slm, knit to end.

Row 3, Dec Row: Knit to m, slm, work Row 1 of Garter Ridge St to last 3 sts, p2tog tbl, k1—1 st dec'd.

Row 4: K1, work Row 2 of Garter Ridge St to m, slm, knit to end.

Row 5, Dec Row: Rep Row 1—108 (113, 117, 119, 121, 123, 125) sts rem.

Row 6: Rep Row 2.

Work Rows 1–4 of Garter Ridge St 7 (10, 10, 10, 10, 11, 12) times without decreasing further, then rep Rows 1 and 2 once more.

Neck should meas about 4½ (6, 6, 6, 6, 6½, 7)" (10 [15, 15, 15, 15, 16.5, 18] cm) from center st BO.

RIGHT NECK SHAPING

Row 1, Inc Row: (RS) Knit to m, slm, work Row 3 of Garter Ridge St to last st, M1R, k1—1 st inc'd.

Row 2: K1, work Row 4 of Garter Ridge St to m, slm, knit to end.

Row 3, Inc Row: Knit to m, slm, work Row 1 of Garter Ridge St to last st, M1P, k1—1 st inc'd.

Row 4: K1, work Row 2 of Garter Ridge St to m, slm, knit to end.

Row 5: Rep Row 1—111 (116, 120, 133, 124, 126, 128) sts.

Row 6: K1, work Row 4 of Garter Ridge St to m, slm, knit to end.

Row 7: Knit to m, slm, work Row 1 of Garter Ridge St to last st, k1.

Break yarn. Place Back sts onto st holder or waste yarn.

front

Return 111 (116, 120, 133, 124, 126, 128) held Front sts to needles and rejoin yarn at neck edge with RS facing.

LEFT NECK SHAPING

Row 1: (RS) BO 4 sts, work Row 3 of Garter Ridge St to m, slm, knit to end—107 (112, 116, 118, 120, 122, 124) sts rem.

Row 2: (WS) Knit to m, sl m, work Row 4 of Garter Ridge St to last st, k1.

Row 3, Dec Row: K1, p2tog, work Row 1 of Garter Ridge St to m, slm, knit to end—106 (111, 115, 117, 119, 121, 123) sts rem.

Row 4: Knit to m, slm, work row 2 of Garter Ridge St to last st, k1.

Row 5, Dec Row: K1, ssk, work Row 3 of Garter Ridge St to m, slm, knit to end—105 (110, 114, 116, 118, 120, 122) sts rem.

Row 6: Knit to m, slm, work Row 4 of Garter Ridge St to last st, k1.

Work Rows 1–4 of Garter Ridge St 7 (10, 10, 10, 10, 11, 12) times without decreasing further, then rep Rows 1 and 2 once more.

RIGHT NECK SHAPING

Row 1, Inc Row: K1, M1R, work Row 3 of Garter Ridge St to m, slm, knit to end—106 (111, 115, 117, 119, 121, 123) sts.

Row 2: Knit to m, slm, work Row 4 of Garter Ridge St to last st, k1.

Row 3, Inc Row: K1, M1P, work Row 1 of Garter Ridge St to m, slm, knit to end—107 (112, 116, 118, 120, 122, 124) sts.

Row 4: Knit to m, slm, work Row 2 of Garter Ridge St to last st, k1.

Row 5: (RS) Use the Backward Loop method (see Glossary) to CO 4 sts, work Row 3 of Garter Ridge St to m, slm, knit to end—111 (116, 120, 133, 124, 126, 128) sts.

Row 6: Knit to m, slm, work Row 4 of Garter Ridge St to last st, k1.

Row 7: K1, work Row 1 of Garter Ridge St to m, slm, knit to end.

REJOIN FRONT AND BACK

Next Row: (WS) Knit to m, slm, work Row 2 of Garter Ridge St to end, use the Backward Loop method to CO 1 st and mark for center st with removable marker, return 111 (116, 120, 133, 124, 126, 128) Back sts to needle and cont working Row 2 of Garter Ridge St to m, slm, knit to end—223 (233, 241, 245, 249, 253, 257) sts.

right body

Next Row: (RS) Knit to m, slm, work Row 3 of Garter Ridge St to m, slm, knit to end.

Work even in Garter Ridge St, knitting the first and last 10 sts of each row, until piece meas 3¾ (4¼, 5¼, 6¼, 7¼, 7¾, 8¾)" (9.5 [11, 13.5, 16, 18.5, 19.5, 22] cm) from join and ending after Row 4 of Garter Ridge St patt.

SHAPE RIGHT SHOULDER

Rows 1 and 2: Knit to m, slm, purl to m, slm, knit to end.

Row 3, Dec Row: (RS) Knit to 1 st before center st, sl2, k1, p2sso, knit to end—2 sts dec'd.

Row 4: Knit to m, slm, purl to m, knit to end.

Rep last 4 rows 2 more times, then rep Rows 1 and 2 once more—217 (227, 235, 239, 243, 247, 251) sts rem.

BIND OFF BODY

Next Row: (RS) BO 68 (71, 73, 73, 73, 73, 73) sts for side seam, knit to 1 st before center st, sl2, k1, p2sso removing center m, knit to end, turn, BO 68 (71, 73, 73, 73, 73, 73) sts for side seam—79 (83, 87, 91, 95, 99, 103) sts rem.

right sleeve

Next Row: (WS) K1, work Row 4 of Garter Ridge St to last st, k1.

Sizes 38 (46, 50, 58)" (96.5 [117, 127, 147.5] cm) Only
Work Rows 1–4 of Garter Ridge St as est, knitting the first and last st of every row 1 (2, 1, 5) time(s), then work 2 (3, 2, 2) more rows.

SHAPE SLEEVE

Dec Row: K1, k2tog on knit rows or p2tog tbl on purl rows, work in patt as est to last 3 sts, ssk on knit rows or p2tog on purl rows, k1—2 sts dec'd.

Work 5 (5, 5, 4, 4, 4, 3) rows even in patt as est.

Rep the last 6 (6, 6, 5, 5, 5, 4) rows 12 (11, 12, 12, 13, 15, 14) more times—55 (61, 63, 67, 69, 69, 75) sts rem.

Next Row: Rep Dec Row—53 (59, 61, 65, 67, 67, 73) sts rem.

Work 1 (1, 1, 3, 3, 3, 1) row(s) in Garter Ridge St as est, maintaining the first and last sts in Garter St, ending after Row 4 of patt.

EST CUFF PATT

Work 3 (3, 3, 0, 0, 0, 1) row(s) even in Broken Seed St.

Rep Dec Row—2 sts dec'd.

Work 5 (5, 5, 4, 4, 4, 3) rows in Broken Seed St.

A: 8¼ (9½, 10, 10, 10½, 10½, 11)"
21 [24, 25.5, 25.5, 26.5, 26.5, 28] cm)

B: 16¼ (16¼, 16¼, 16¼, 16¼, 16¾, 16¾)"
41.5 [41.5, 41.5, 41.5, 41.5, 42.5, 42.5] cm)

C: 15 (15¾, 16¼, 16¼, 16¼, 16¼, 16¼)"
38 [40, 41.5, 41.5, 41.5, 41.5, 41.5] cm)

D: 17½ (18½, 19¼, 20¼, 21, 22, 23)"
44.5 [47, 49, 51.5, 53.5, 56, 58.5] cm)

E: 33 (38, 42, 46, 50, 53, 58)"
84 [96.5, 106.5, 117, 127, 134.5, 147.5] cm)

F: 14 (17, 17½, 17½, 18, 18½, 19)"
35.5 [43, 44.5, 44.5, 45.5, 47, 48.5] cm)

G: 7" (18 cm)

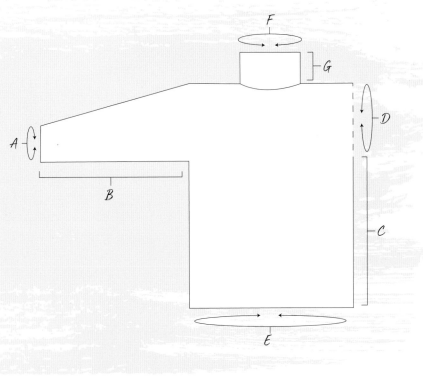

Rep the last 6 (6, 6, 5, 5, 5, 4) rows 6 (6, 6, 8, 8, 8, 10) more times—39 (45, 47, 47, 49, 49, 51) sts rem.

Rep Inc Row once more—37 (43, 45, 45, 47, 47, 49) sts rem.

Next Row: (WS) Knit.

BO all sts loosely.

collar

Using Crochet Provisional Cast-on method (see Glossary) and waste yarn, CO 32 sts. Change to working yarn and cir needle. Do not join; work back and forth in rows.

Row 1: (RS) K16, pm, k16.

Row 2: (WS) Knit to m, slm, purl to last st, k1.

Row 3: K1, work Row 1 of Garter Ridge St to m, slm, knit to end.

Row 4: Knit to m, slm, work Row 2 of Garter Ridge St to last st, k1.

Row 5: K1, work Row 3 of Garter Ridge St to m, slm, knit to end.

Row 6: Knit to m, slm, work Row 2 of Garter Ridge St to last st, k1.

Rep last 4 rows 27 (33, 34, 34, 35, 36, 37) more times, then rep Rows 3 and 4 once more.

Break yarn and place sts onto waste yarn.

finishing

Block sweater and collar flat to measurements.

ATTACH COLLAR

Once dry, remove provisional cast-on from collar and graft the cast-on sts to the held sts using the Kitchener Stitch (see Glossary). Fold the collar so that the Garter St side is on the back and the Garter Ridge side is on the front or RS facing. Seam the collar to the sweater neckline, carefully matching ridges at the center front neckline, working around to the center back on each side.

Seam sleeves and sides together using preferred method, starting at the cuff of the sleeve and ending at the hem of the body.

Weave in ends.

y o t h
yarns

With my dedication to finding yarn that fit within certain fiber contents and colors, YOTH Yarns made the task a joy. Working with a family business is always a joy, too, and the company's founder, Veronika—who goes by both Ve and Big Sister—put her brother Danny (aka Little Brother) in the hot seat for our glimpse into YOTH Yarns.

It might be a cliché, but it all started with a dream. YOTH Yarns was born of Veronika's passion for knitting and her desire to create a career where she could be creative and fulfilled in what she did. Many years ago, Ve ran a blog called Yarn On The House, hence the name YOTH, in the hopes of someday transitioning into the yarn industry in some way. In those days, YOTH was only a little seed, but in those moments of interviewing talented designers and small indie yarn dyeing companies, Ve realized she wanted to develop a small business of her own.

Working a brain-numbing corporate job, she approached her family with her business plan. Little Brother, who she can't ever imagine running the business without, became her business partner. Ve's husband, Marc, became the backbone of the company's online existence. Their parents, who have always been Little Bro's and Big Sis's rocks, and all of the many friends and other family members who pitched in whenever and wherever they could, became a much-valued support system. It's one big happy family business—not without its challenges and squabbles, but they wouldn't trade it for anything.

Their big mission and goal is to produce not only a quality product that keeps them wanting to knit, but also a product that is proudly created and manufactured in the U.S. to the fullest extent possible. All of YOTH Yarn's bases are milled and spun in North America, with the majority made Stateside; most of the fibers come from sheep who roam American lands, and all of the yarns are cleaned and dyed at a beautiful dye house in Maine, then distributed and shipped from a little warehouse on the family property in Carnation, Washington. The array of fibers and yarns that YOTH Yarns offers has grown and the company continues to learn from the knitting community as it builds and earns its place in the market.

WHY BIG SISTER?

Qui is one of those pullovers that I would consider daily wear. In the fall, I want a simple pullover that's not fussy to style, has a casual fit, and feels cozy, with room to layer. However, simplicity can easily slide into the rut of boring, so having a yarn with crisp stitch definition that would wear well without losing shape was extremely important to me. On my journey of seeking out independents and companies with strong ethics and values, I found it challenging to also find a dependable, workhorse yarn, but all of the yarns I've worked with from YOTH have been just that. Big Sister is the perfect medium-weight, round, balanced yarn for every knitter and every day. The choice was a simple one.

YOTH Yarns is a knockout at craft events because of the sheer variety in product color. People liken it to a woolly candy store with rows and rows of options. I was looking for a green yarn for Qui, but I didn't find just light green or dark green—there was bluish and yellowish and bright and muted, across every part of the value spectrum.

cormac

cardi

Gaelic; son of the raven

This tidy little cardigan is worked from the top down and features rag-lan shaping accented with cables, while the shoulders have contrast-ing cables that run the length of the sleeves. The front pieces house Garter Stitch panels to accentuate the shape, and hidden pockets are worked into the side seams. This classic raglan is relaxed and casual and suits many body types—a wardrobe staple with details throughout that make it special and unique.

Finished Sizes
16¼ (18, 19, 20¾, 21¾, 23½, 25, 26¾, 28)" (41.5 [45.5, 48.5, 52.5, 55, 59.5, 63.5, 68, 71] cm) across back at underarms.

Designed to fit 30 (33, 36, 39, 42, 45, 48, 51, 54)" (76 [84, 91.5, 99, 106.5, 114.5, 122, 129.5, 137] cm) bust, with 1½–3" (4–7.5 cm) added for ease.

Sweater shown measures 19" (48.5 cm) across back and fits a 36" (91.5 cm) bust.

Yarn
Worsted weight (#4 Medium)

Shown here: Amano Warmi (70% baby alpaca, 30% Merino wool; 164 yd

[150 m]/3½ oz [100 g]): #6003 Quinoa, 6 (7, 7, 8, 8, 9, 10, 10, 11) hanks.

Needles
Size U.S. 8 (5 mm): 24" (60) circular (cir), set of 4 or 5 double-pointed (dpn).

Size U.S. H/8 (5 mm) crochet hook for provisional cast-on.

Adjust needle size if necessary to obtain the correct gauge.

Notions
Markers (m); cable needle (cn); stitch holders; yarn needle.

Gauge
18 sts and 27 rows = 4" (10 cm) in St st worked flat, blocked.

Notes
⤳ The cardigan is worked flat from the top down in one piece. The neckband is worked as a long strip, stitches are picked up and knit along the edge, and the yoke shaping begins. The cable patterns and neckband are worked throughout and will continue when pattern directions state to work in patt as est.

⤳ Circular needle is used to accommodate large number of sts. Do not turn; work back and forth in rows.

⤳ Pockets are worked into the sides of the body using a double increase starting just below the underarm. When the pocket is increased to the desired size, the sts are bound off, forming the bottom of the pocket.

92

Stitch Guide

NECKBAND PANEL (PANEL OF 9 STS)
Row 1: (RS) K3, p1, k1, p1, k3.

Row 2: (WS) K4, p1, k4.

Rep Rows 1 and 2 for patt.

LATERAL BRAID
*Knit into the back of the second st on the LH needle, then knit the first st on the LH needle and drop both sts off at once. Transfer the first st on the RH needle back to the LH needle; rep from * to end.

neckband

With crochet hook and waste yarn, use Crochet Provisional Cast-on method (see Glossary) to CO 9 sts.

With cir needle and working yarn, work Rows 1 and 2 of Neckband Panel (see Stitch Guide) 47 (53, 56, 59, 60, 60, 62, 66, 68) times, then rep Row 1 once more. Do not turn after last row.

yoke

Pick-up Row: (RS) Rotate work clockwise, pick up and knit 47 (53, 56, 59, 60, 60, 62, 66, 68) sts along neckband edge, remove waste yarn from provisional CO and place 9 sts onto empty needle, k3, p1, k1, p1, k3—65 (71, 74, 77, 78, 78, 80, 84, 86) sts.

EST RAGLAN CHARTS
Next Row: (WS) Work in patt as est over first 9 sts, work Raglan Right Chart, placing markers as indicated on chart, pm, k7 (13, 16, 19, 20, 20, 22, 26, 28) across Back, work Raglan Left Chart, placing markers as indicated on chart to last 9 sts, work in patt as est to end—11 sts each Front, 8 sts each Sleeve, and 27 (33, 36, 39, 40, 40, 42, 46, 48) sts for Back.

SHAPE RAGLAN
Work Neckband Panel and Raglan Right and Left Charts as est, working Back sts in St st through WS Row 35 of charts, and placing 2 markers on Row 18 as indicated—201 (207, 210, 213, 214, 214, 216, 220, 222) sts; 28 sts each Front, 42 sts each Sleeve, and 61 (67, 70, 73, 74, 74, 76, 80, 82) sts for Back.

EST FRONT CONTINUED CHARTS
Next Row: (RS) Work 9 sts in Neckband Panel as est, work Front Right Continued Chart, cont in patt as est, working all raglan inc as est to last 28 sts, work Front Left Continued Chart to last 9 sts, work in Neckband Panel as est to end—209 (215, 218, 221, 222, 222, 224, 228, 230) sts; 29 sts each Front, 44 sts each Sleeve, and 63 (69, 72, 75, 76, 76, 78, 82, 84) sts for Back.

Work through Row 41 (43, 45, 49, 53, 61, 65, 69, 73) of Continued Charts—225 (239, 250, 269, 286, 318, 336, 356, 374) sts; 31 (32, 33, 35, 37, 41, 43, 45, 47) sts each Front, 48 (50, 52, 56, 60, 68, 72, 76, 80) sts each Sleeve, and 67 (75, 80, 87, 92, 100, 106, 114, 120) sts for Back.

Front Inc Row: (RS) Work in patt as est to first m, M1R, slm, work in patt as est without inc raglan further and remove markers to last m, slm, M1L, work in patt as est to end—2 sts inc'd.

Next Row: (WS) Work in patt as est to end.

Rep last 2 rows 2 (2, 2, 1, 1, 0, 0, 0, 0) more time(s)—231 (245, 256, 273, 290, 320, 338, 358, 376) sts; 34 (35, 36, 37, 39, 42, 44, 46, 48) sts each Front, 48 (50, 52, 56, 60, 68, 72, 76, 80) sts each Sleeve, and 67 (75, 80, 87, 92, 100, 106, 114, 120) sts for Back.

DIVIDE BODY AND SLEEVES
Next Row: (RS) Work in patt as est to first m, M1R, slm, work next 10 sts in patt as est, place contrasting m, use the Backward Loop method (see Glossary) to CO 3 sts, CO 1 st and mark for side st, CO 3 more sts for right underarm, transfer next 48 (50, 52, 56, 60, 68, 72, 76, 80) sts onto st holder or waste yarn for Sleeve, place contrasting m, cont across Back in patt as est, place contrasting m, CO 3 sts, CO 1 st and mark for side st, CO 3 more sts for left underarm, transfer next 48 (50, 52, 56, 60, 68, 72, 76, 80) sts onto st holder or waste yarn for Sleeve, place contrasting m, work in patt as est to m, slm, M1L, work in patt as est to end—151 (161, 168, 177, 186, 200, 210, 222, 232) sts; 7 sts between contrasting markers on each side.

RAGLAN RIGHT CHART

☐ knit on RS, purl on WS

• purl on RS, knit on WS

mR make 1 right

mL make 1 left

| marker position

⤬ sl 1 onto cn, hold in
   back, k1, k1 from cn

⤬ sl 1 st onto cn, hold in
   front, k1, k1 from cn

⤬ sl 3 onto cn, hold in
   back, k3, k3 from cn

⤬ sl 3 st onto cn, hold in
   front, k3, k3 from cn

☐ repeat these rows
   when pattern is continued
   beyond charts

FRONT RIGHT CONTINUED CHART

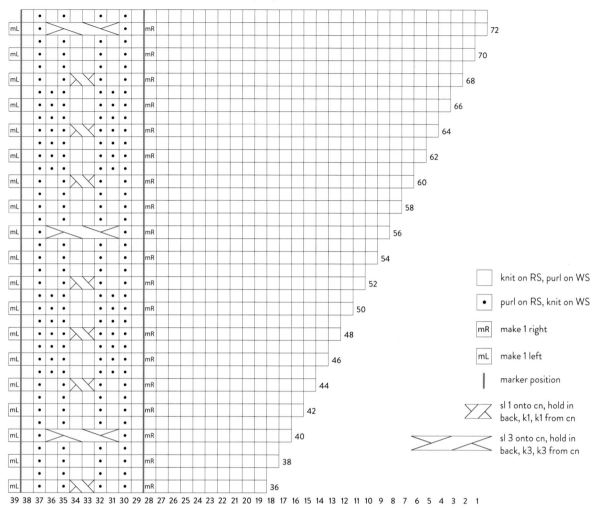

	knit on RS, purl on WS
•	purl on RS, knit on WS
mR	make 1 right
mL	make 1 left
│	marker position
	sl 1 onto cn, hold in back, k1, k1 from cn
	sl 3 onto cn, hold in back, k3, k3 from cn

body

SHAPE FRONTS, POCKETS & EST GARTER RIDGE PATT

Row 1: (WS) Work in patt as est to first contrasting m, slm, purl to m, slm, work in patt as est to next contrasting m, slm, purl to m, slm, work in patt as est to end.

Row 2, Inc Row: (RS) Work in patt as est to 1 st before m, p1, M1R, slm, *work in patt as est to contrasting m, slm, purl to m, slm; rep from * once more, work in patt as est to m, slm, M1L, p1, work in patt as est to end—2 sts inc'd.

Note: For all Row 2 reps, inc the number of purl sts before M1R on Right Front and after M1L on Left Front by 2 sts.

*For example, the next rep of Row 2 would be worked as: Work in patt as est to 3 sts before m, p3, M1R, slm, *work in patt as est to contrasting m, slm, purl to m, slm; rep from * once more, work in patt as est to m, slm, M1L, p3, work in patt as est to end.)*

Row 3: Work Neckband Panel as est, purl to m, slm, *work in patt as est to contrasting m, slm, purl to m, slm; rep from * once more, work in patt as est to m, purl to last 9 sts, work in Neckband Panel as est to end.

Row 4, Inc Row: Work Neckband Panel as est, knit to m, M1R, slm, *work in patt as est to contrasting m, slm, knit to side st, k1, yo, k1 into st, knit to m, slm; rep from * once more, work in patt as est to m, M1L, knit to last 9 sts, work Neckband Panel as est to end—4 sts inc'd.

Rep last 4 rows 17 (17, 17, 18, 18, 19, 19, 20, 20) more times, then rep through Row 1 (1, 3, 3, 3, 1, 3, 3, 3) once more—259 (269, 278, 293, 302, 320, 332, 350, 360) sts; 43 (43, 43, 45, 45, 47, 47, 49, 49) sts between contrasting markers on each side.

Piece should meas about 10¾ (10¾, 11, 11½, 11½, 12, 12¼, 12¾, 12¾)" (27.5 [27.5, 28, 29, 29, 30.5, 31, 32.5, 32.5] cm) from underarm.

RAGLAN LEFT CHART

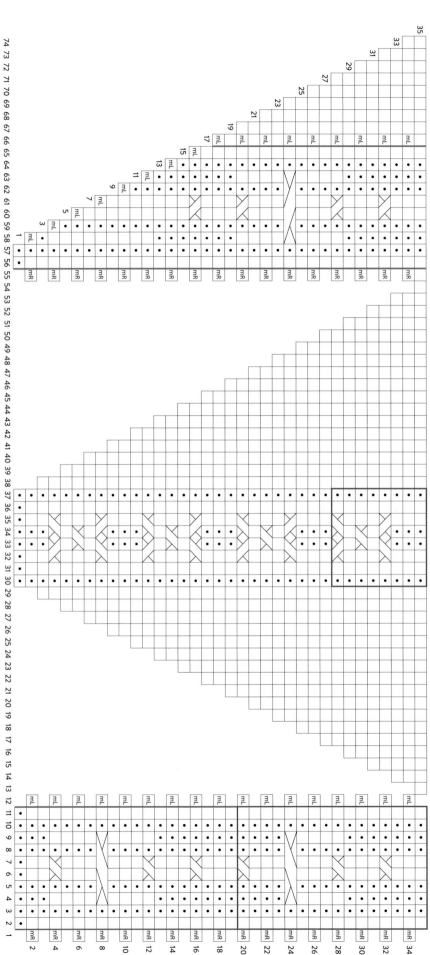

knit on RS, purl on WS

• purl on RS, knit on WS

mR make 1 right

mL make 1 left

| marker position

sl 1 onto cn, hold in
back, k1, k1 from cn

sl 1 st onto cn, hold in
front, k1, k1 from cn

sl 3 onto cn, hold in
back, k3, k3 from cn

sl 3 st onto cn, hold in
front, k3, k3 from cn

repeat these rows
when pattern is continued
beyond charts

FRONT LEFT CONTINUED CHART

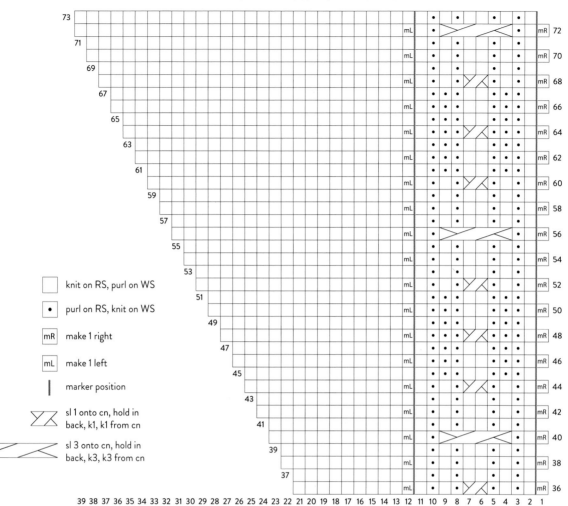

knit on RS, purl on WS

• purl on RS, knit on WS

mR make 1 right

mL make 1 left

| marker position

sl 1 onto cn, hold in back, k1, k1 from cn

sl 3 onto cn, hold in back, k3, k3 from cn

Pocket Inc Row: (RS) Work in patt as est to m, M1R, slm, *work in patt as est to first contrasting m, slm, k3, [kfb] to 3 sts before next contrasting m, k3, slm; rep from * once more, work in patt as est to m, M1L, work in patt as est to end—335 (345, 354, 373, 382, 404, 416, 438, 448) sts; 80 (80, 80, 84, 84, 88, 88, 92, 92) sts between contrasting markers on each side.

Next Row: (WS) Work in patt as est to end.

BIND OFF POCKET

Next Row: (RS) Work in patt as est to m, M1R, slm, *work in patt as est to first contrasting m, slm, work 3 sts, BO 74 (74, 74, 78, 78, 82, 82, 86, 86) pocket sts, until 3 sts rem before next contrasting m, work 3 sts, slm; rep from * once more, work in patt as est to m, slm, M1L, p1, work in patt as est to end—189 (199, 208, 219, 228, 242, 254, 268, 278) sts rem; 6 sts rem between contrasting markers on each side.

Inc Row: (WS) *Work in patt as est to contrasting m, slm, work 3 sts, use the Backward Loop method to CO 1 st, work 3 sts, slm; rep from * once more, work in patt as est to end—191 (201, 210, 221, 230, 244, 256, 270, 280) sts; 7 sts between contrasting markers on each side.

Work even in patt as est for 4 more rows, cont to inc each RS row at front bands only—195 (205, 214, 225, 234, 248, 260, 274, 284) sts.

HEM

Row 1: (RS) K3, p1, k1, p1, knit to last 6 sts, p1, k1, p1, k3.

Row 2: (WS) K4, p1, knit to last 5 sts, p1, k4.

Rep last 2 rows 2 more times.

Next Row: K4, work Lateral Braid (see Stitch Guide) to last 4 sts, k4.

Knit 5 rows and BO loosely.

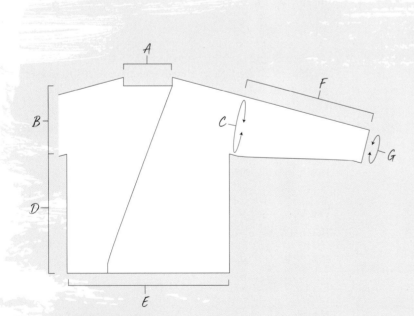

A: 6 (7¼, 8, 8¾, 9, 9, 9¼, 10¼, 10¾) "
15 [18.5, 20.5, 22, 23, 23, 23.5, 26, 27.5] cm)

B: 7 (7¼, 7½, 7¾, 8½, 9¼, 10, 10½, 11)"
18 [18.5, 19, 19.5, 21.5, 23.5, 25.5, 26.5, 28] cm

C: 12¼ (12¾, 13, 14, 15, 16¾, 17½, 18½, 19¼)"
31 [32.5, 33, 35.5, 38, 42.5, 44.5, 47, 49] cm)

D: 13¾ (13¾, 14, 14¾, 14¾, 15, 15¼, 15¾, 15¾)"
35 [35, 35.5, 37.5, 37.5, 38, 38.5, 40, 40] cm

E: 16¼ (18, 19, 20¾, 21¾, 23½, 25, 26¾, 28)"
41.5 [45.5, 48.5, 52.5, 55, 59.5, 63.5, 68, 71] cm)

F: 17 (17, 17, 17½, 17½, 17½, 17½, 17½, 17½)"
43 [43, 43, 44.5, 44.5, 44.5, 44.5, 44.5, 44.5] cm)

G: 7¼ (7¾, 7¾, 8¼, 8¼, 8¼, 8¾, 8¾, 8¾)"
18.5 [19.5, 19.5, 21, 21, 21, 22, 22, 22] cm)

sleeves

Note: *Work the cable panel down the center the same as on the Raglan Right and Left charts, repeating only the rows outlined in red.)*

Return 48 (50, 52, 56, 60, 68, 72, 76, 80) held sts from one sleeve to dpns. Beg at center of underarm and with RS facing, pick up and knit 4 sts, work to end of held sts as est, pick up and knit last 3 underarm sts, pm, and join for rnds—55 (57, 59, 63, 67, 75, 79, 83, 87) sts.

Work 8 (8, 7, 7, 5, 4, 4, 3, 3) rnds even in patt as est.

Dec Rnd: K1, k2tog, work in patt as est to last 2 sts, ssk—2 sts dec'd.

Rep last 9 (9, 8, 8, 6, 5, 5, 4, 4) rnds 10 (10, 11, 12, 14, 18, 19, 21, 23) more times—33 (35, 35, 37, 37, 37, 39, 39, 39) sts rem.

Work even in patt as est until sleeve meas 15½ (15½, 15½, 16, 16, 16, 16, 16, 16)" (39.5 [39.5, 39.5, 40.5, 40.5, 40.5, 40.5, 40.5, 40.5] cm) from underarm.

CUFF

Knit 1 rnd.

Purl 1 rnd.

Rep last 2 rnds 2 more times.

Next Rnd: Work Lateral Braid to end.

Purl 1 rnd.

Knit 1 rnd.

Rep last 2 rnds once more.

Purl 1 rnd.

BO loosely.

finishing

Seam pockets and tack corner of pocket to inside of cardigan front. Weave in ends and block to measurements.

h a z a n
d o l m a n

Turkish; born in autumn

A poncho-style sweater is perfect for chilly autumn days. Small bead details and textured stitches under the loft and fluff of the yarn, paired with clean, folded hems, come together to make an extremely cozy sweater that is easy to style. The generous ease flatters a wide variety of body types, and the selective detail makes it appropriate for many ages.

Finished Size
42 (44, 46, 48, 50, 52, 54, 56, 58, 60, 62)" (106.5 [112, 117, 122, 127, 132, 137, 142, 147.5, 152.5, 157.5] cm) bust circumference.

Designed to fit 30 (32, 34, 36, 38, 40, 42, 44, 46, 48, 50)" (76 [81.5, 86.5, 91.5, 96.5, 101.5, 106.5, 112, 117, 122, 127] cm) bust, with 12" (30.5 cm) added for ease.

Sweater shown measures 48" (122 cm) and fits a 36" (91.5 cm) bust.

Yarn
DK weight (#3 Light).

Shown here: Blue Sky Fibers Brushed Suri (67% baby suri alpaca, 22% fine Merino wool, 11% bamboo: 142 yd [130 m]/1¾ oz [50 g]): #900 Whipped Cream, 5 (5, 6, 6, 7, 7, 8, 8, 9, 9, 10) hanks.

Needles
Size U.S. 8 (5 mm): 16" and 32" (40 and 80 cm) circular (cir).

Adjust needle size if necessary to obtain the correct gauge.

Notions
Markers (m); stitch holders or waste yarn; bead needle or small crochet hook; yarn needle; 30 size 6 mm or 9 mm beads with large hole.

Gauge
18 sts and 24 rnds = 4" (10 cm) in St st.

Notes
‚ÄÈ The beadwork details are extremely easy to execute, but it may be useful to practice the technique on a swatch before working on the final piece.

‚ÄÈ Sleeves are picked up and knit from the armhole, worked flat, and seamed in finishing.

‚ÄÈ If using the suggested yarn, the neckband may be too tight if using an alternate method for seaming the neckband; the sewn bind-off yields the best results.

REVERSE BROKEN RIB (MULTIPLE OF 2 STS + 1)

Row 1: (WS) Knit.

Row 2: (RS) *K1, p1; rep from * to last st, k1.

Rep Rows 1 and 2 for patt. Work Row 2 as foll to maintain patt during sleeve shaping:

After Inc Row: K2, *p1, k1; rep from * to last st, k1.

After next Inc Row, rep Row 2.

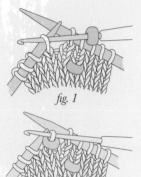

fig. 1

fig. 2

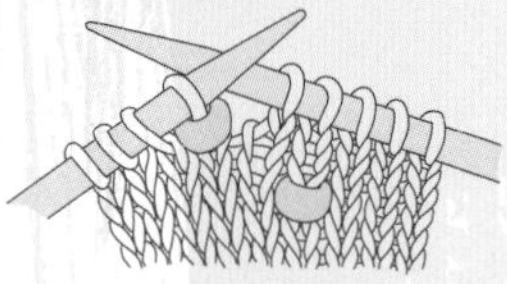

fig. 3

BEAD 1

1. Insert crochet hook or bead needle through bead, hook next st on LH needle (*fig. 1*).

2. Pull st through bead (*fig. 2*).

3. Place st back onto LH needle (*fig. 3*).

4. Knit the stitch with the bead in place.

body

Using longer needles, CO 189 (198, 207, 216, 225, 234, 243, 252, 261, 270, 279) sts. Pm for beg of rnd and and join for working in the rnd, being careful not to twist sts.

Knit 10 rnds.

Turning Rnd: Purl.

Knit 10 rnds.

Fold along turning rnd and knit each st together with corresponding CO st to create hem.

Knit until piece meas 4 ¼" (11 cm) from hem edge.

Sizes 42 (46, 50, 54, 58, 62)" (106.5 [117, 127, 137, 147.5, 157.5] cm) Only

Inc Rnd: Kfb, knit to end—190 (208, 226, 244, 262, 280) sts.

Sizes 44 (48, 52, 56, 60)" (112 [122, 132, 142, 152.5] cm) Only

Next Rnd: Knit.

SHAPE SIDES

Inc Rnd: *K1, M1L, k93 (97, 102, 106, 111, 115, 120, 124, 129, 133, 138), M1R, k1, pm; rep from * once more—4 sts inc'd.

Next Rnd: Knit.

Inc Rnd: *K1, M1L, knit to 1 st before m, M1R, k1, slm; rep from * once more—4 sts inc'd.

Rep last 2 rnds 3 more times—210 (218, 228, 236, 246, 254, 272, 282, 290, 300) sts.

DIVIDE FOR UNDERARMS

Next Rnd: BO 5, knit to 5 sts before m, BO 10 for left underarm, knit to last 5 sts, BO 5 finishing right underarm—95 (99, 104, 108, 113, 117, 122, 126, 131, 135, 140) sts rem each back and front.

Break yarn and set Body sts aside, keeping sts on cir needle.

sleeves (make 2)

Using shorter needles, CO 37 (37, 37, 39, 41, 41, 41, 41, 41, 43, 43). Do not join; work back and forth in rows.

SHAPE SLEEVE

Work Reverse Broken Rib (see Stitch Guide) for 17 (11, 9, 9, 9, 7, 5, 3, 3, 3, 3) rows.

Inc Row: (RS) K1, M1L, work in patt to last st, M1R, k1—2 sts inc'd.

Rep last 18 (12, 10, 10, 10, 8, 6, 4, 4, 4, 4) rows 2 (3, 4, 4, 4, 6, 7, 10, 11, 12, 13) more times, working inc'd sts in patt as they become available—43 (45, 47, 49, 51, 55, 57, 63, 65, 69, 71) sts.

Work even in Reverse Broken Rib until piece meas 9¾ (9¾, 10, 10¼, 10½, 10½, 10½, 10½, 10½, 10½, 10½)" (25 [25, 25.5, 26, 26.5, 26.5, 26.5, 26.5, 26.5, 26.5, 26.5] cm) from CO edge, ending after a RS row.

Next Row: (WS) BO 5, knit to last 5 sts, BO 5—33 (35, 37, 39, 41, 45, 47, 53, 55, 59, 61) sts rem.

Break yarn. Place all sleeve sts onto a st holder or waste yarn.

yoke

With RS facing, join sleeves to body as foll:

Joining Rnd: Using longer cir needle attached to Body, k33 (35, 37, 39, 41, 45, 47, 53, 55, 59, 61) right Sleeve sts, pm, k95 (99, 104, 108, 113, 117, 122, 126, 131, 135, 140) Body sts for Back, pm, k33 (35, 37, 39, 41, 45, 47, 53, 55, 59, 61) left Sleeve sts, pm, k95 (99, 104, 108, 113, 117, 122, 126, 131, 135, 140) rem Body sts for Front, place contrasting marker for new beg of rnd—256 (268, 282, 294, 308, 324, 338, 358, 372, 388, 402) sts.

Knit 1 rnd.

EST BEADING

Rnd 1: *K8 (9, 10, 11, 12, 14, 15, 18, 19, 21, 22), work 17 sts in Bead Chart, [knit to next m, sl m] 2 times; rep from * once more.

Cont working as est for 12 more rows, ending after Rnd 14 of Bead Chart.

SHAPE FRONT

Dec Rnd: [Knit to m, slm] 3 times, ssk, knit to last 2 sts, k2tog—2 sts dec'd.

Knit 1 rnd.

Beads placed at the elbows take this design from chic to spectacular.

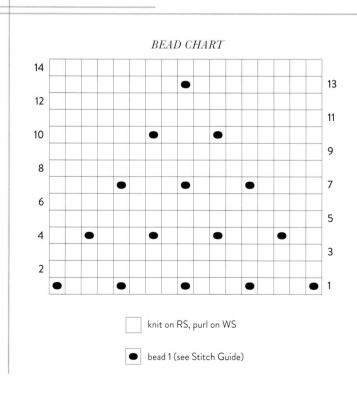

BEAD CHART

knit on RS, purl on WS

● bead 1 (see Stitch Guide)

Rep last 2 rnds 3 more times—248 (260, 274, 286, 300, 316, 330, 350, 364, 380, 394) sts. On last rnd, remove all markers except beg-of-rnd m.

SHAPE YOKE

| **Note:** *It may be helpful to use a pencil to circle the instructions for your size. Be aware that the placement of the numbers in relationship to the ( ) may change when only some sizes are worked.*

Sizes 42 (44, 48, 50, 52, 54, 56, 58, 60, 62)"
(106.5 [112, 122, 127, 132, 137, 142, 147.5, 152.5, 157.5] cm) Only
Dec Rnd 1: K2 (2, 3, 3, 3, 3, 3, 3, 4, 4), [k2tog, k4 (4, 4, 4, 4, 6, 6, 6, 6, 6)] 9 (15, 18, 11, 3, 4, 14, 21, 17, 10) times, [k2tog, k3 (3, 5, 5, 5, 5, 5, 5, 5, 7, 7)] 27 (15, 9, 23, 39, 37, 17, 3, 11, 25) times, [k2tog, k4 (4, 4, 4, 4, 6, 6, 6, 6, 6)] 9 (15, 18, 11, 3, 4, 14, 21, 17, 10) times, k2tog, k1 (1, 2, 2, 2, 2, 2, 2, 3, 3)—202 (214, 240, 254, 270, 284, 304, 318, 334, 348) sts rem.

Size 46" (117 cm) Only
Dec Rnd 1: *K2, [k2tog, k4] 22 times, k2tog, k1; rep from * once more—228 sts rem.

All Sizes
Knit until piece meas 7¾ (7¾, 8, 8¼, 8½, 8½, 8½, 8½, 8½, 8½, 8½)" (19.5 [19.5, 20.5, 21, 21.5, 21.5, 21.5, 21.5, 21.5, 21.5, 21.5] cm) from joining rnd.

Sizes 42 (44, 50, 52, 58, 60)"
(106.5 [112, 127, 132, 147.5, 152.5] cm) Only
Dec Rnd 2: *K3 (1, 1, 1, 1, 1), [k2tog, k2] 24 (26, 31, 33, 39, 41) times, k2tog; rep from * once more—152 (160, 190, 202, 238, 250) sts rem.

Sizes 46 (54, 62)" (117 [137, 157.5] cm) Only
Dec Rnd 2: K1, [k2tog, k2] 27 (34, 42) times, [k2tog, k1] 3 times, [k2tog, k2] 27 (34, 42) times, k2tog—170 (212, 260) sts rem.

Sizes 48 and 56" (122 and 142 cm) Only
Dec Rnd 2: K1, *k2tog, k2; rep from * to last 3 sts, k2tog, k1—180 (228) sts rem.

All Sizes
Knit until piece meas 13¼ (13½, 13¾, 14, 14½, 14¾, 15, 15¼, 15¼, 15½, 15½)" (33.5 [34.5, 35, 35.5, 37, 37.5, 38, 38.5, 38.5, 39.5, 39.5] cm) from joining rnd.

Sizes 42 (46, 54, 62)" (106.5 [117, 137, 157.5] cm) Only
Dec Rnd 3: K1, k2tog, k2, [k2tog, k1] 47 (53, 67, 83) times, k2tog, k2, k2tog—102 (114, 142, 174) sts rem.

Sizes 44 (50, 52, 58, 60)" (112 [127, 132, 147.5, 152.5] cm) Only
Dec Rnd 3: K1, [k2tog, k2] 2 times, [k2tog, k1] 47 (57, 61, 73, 77) times, [k2tog, k2] 2 times, k2tog—108 (128, 136, 160, 168) sts rem.

Sizes 48 (56)" (122 [142] cm) Only
Dec Rnd 3: *K1, k2tog; rep from * to end—120 (152) sts rem.

All Sizes
Knit until piece meas 15 (16, 16½, 17½, 18, 18½, 18½, 18½, 18½, 19, 19)" (38 [40.5, 42, 44.5, 45.5, 47, 47, 47, 47, 48.5, 48.5] cm) from joining rnd.

SHAPE BACK NECK

> **Note:** *Because of the fuzzy nature of the yarn used in the sample, the gaps created by these short-rows are hidden. If desired, you may slip the first st of Short-rows 2–7 and close the gaps (see Glossary) as you come to them.*

Short-row 1: K34 (35, 37, 38, 40, 42, 44, 46, 48, 50, 52), turn.

Short-row 2: P8, turn.

Short-row 3: K12, turn.

Short-row 4: P16, turn.

Short-row 5: K20, turn.

Short-row 6: P24, turn.

Short-row 7: Knit to end.

Dec Rnd 4: K1, [k2tog] 9 (12, 12, 12, 14, 13, 13, 14, 16, 18, 18) times, (k2tog, k1) 21 (19, 21, 23, 23, 27, 29, 31, 31, 31, 33) times, [k2tog] 10 (13, 13, 13, 15, 14, 14, 15, 17, 19, 19) times—62 (64, 68, 72, 76, 82, 86, 92, 96, 100, 104) sts rem.

neckband

Knit 6 rnds.

Turning Rnd: Purl.

Knit 6 rnds.

Fold along turning rnd and knit each st together with corresponding st along the WS of the fabric to create hem.

BO loosely using the Sewn Bind-off method (see Glossary).

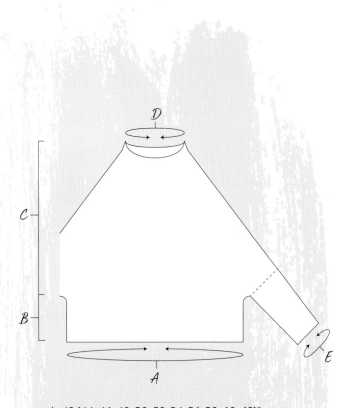

A: 42 (44, 46, 48, 50, 52, 54, 56, 58, 60, 62)" 106.5 [112, 117, 122, 127, 132, 137, 142, 147.5, 152.5, 157.5] cm)

B: 6" (15 cm)

C: 16¼ (17¼, 17¾, 18¾, 19¼, 19¾, 19¾, 19¾, 19¾, 20¼, 20¼)" 41.5 [44, 45, 47.5, 49, 50, 50, 50, 50, 51.5, 51.5] cm)

D: 13¾ (14¼, 15, 16, 17, 18¼, 19, 20½, 21¼, 22¼, 23)" 35 [36, 38, 40.5, 43, 46.5, 48.5, 52, 54, 56.5, 58.5] cm)

E: 8¼ (8¼, 8¼, 8¾, 9, 9, 9, 9, 9, 9½, 9½)" 21 [21, 21, 22, 23, 23, 23, 23, 23, 24, 24] cm)

finishing

Starting at the cuff, seam the sleeves closed. Seam sleeve underarm and body underarm together. Weave in ends and block to measurements.

aki
cowl

Japanese; born in autumn

This cozy, must-have accessory is made using two stitches misunderstood by new knitters, but don't let that deter you! Both brioche and cables are so simple to execute once you "decode" the technique that you'll wonder why you didn't add them to your knitting repertoire long ago. If you've already worked brioche and cables on their own, this cowl is going to be a snap to knit. The suggested yarn is the softest wool you could want against your skin, and the design, with its split hem and ample roominess, results in a versatile piece that can be worn a number of ways.

Finished Size
About 29" (73.5 cm) circumference and 13" (33 cm) long.

Yarn
Worsted weight (#4 Medium).

Shown here: Stone Cormo Worsted (100% American Cormo wool; 200 yd [182 m]/3½ oz [100 g]): #02 Osage, 2 hanks.

Needles
Size U.S. 7 (4.5 mm): 24" (60 cm) circular (cir).

Adjust needle size if necessary to obtain the correct gauge.

Notions
Markers (m); cable needle (cn); stitch holders or waste yarn; yarn needle.

Gauge
16 sts and 20 brioche rows = 4" (10 cm) in Brioche St worked flat.

Notes
⟶ Worked from the bottom up, each flap of the split hem is worked separately, then joined, and the cowl is finished in rnds.

⟶ Because brioche is still gaining momentum, and with the added challenge of cables, each row/round is written line by line rather than written in two row brackets, as you would normally see in a brioche pattern.

⟶ When changing from working flat to working in rounds, the first and last stitch of every other round will be worked as a sl1yo. Be sure each yo is placed correctly around the marker for the beginning of the round.

BRIOCHE STITCH

Worked in Rows (Multiple of 2 sts + 1)

Set-up Row: (WS) *K1, sl1yo; rep from * to last st, k1.

Row 1: (RS) K1, brk, *sl1yo, brk; rep from * to last st, k1.

Row 2: K1, sl1yo, *brk, sl1yo; rep from * to last st, k1.

Rep Rows 1 and 2 for patt.

Worked in Rnds (Multiple of 2 sts)

Rnd 1: *Sl1yo, brk; rep from * to end.

Rnd 2: *Brp, sl1yo; rep from * to end.

Rep Rnds 1 and 2 for patt.

BR2/2RC

Place next 2 sts onto cn and hold to back, brk, sl1yo from LH needle, brk, sl1yo from cn.

BR2/2LC

Place next 2 sts onto cn and hold to front, sl1yo, brk from LH needle, sl1yo, brk from cn.

front hem

CO 57 sts. Do not join.

Work 5 rows in Brioche St (see Stitch Guide), ending after a WS row.

EST CABLE PANEL

Row 1: (RS) K1, [brk, sl1yo] 5 times, pm, [brk, sl1yo] 2 times, BR2/2RC (see Stitch Guide), brk, BR2/2LC (see Stitch Guide), [sl1yo, brk] 2 times, pm, *sl1yo, brk; rep from * to last st, k1.

Rows 2–8: Work 7 rows even in Brioche St, ending after a WS row.

Row 9: K1, [brk, sl1yo] to m, slm, brk, sl1yo, BR2/2RC, [brk, sl1yo] 2 times, brk, BR2/2LC, sl1yo, brk, slm, *sl1yo, brk; rep from * to last st, k1.

Rows 10–16: Work 7 rows even in Brioche St, ending after a WS row.

Row 17: K1, [brk, sl1yo] to m, slm, BR2/2RC, [brk, sl1yo] 4 times, brk, BR2/2LC, slm, *sl1yo, brk; rep from * to last st, k1.

Rows 18–24: Work 7 rows even in Brioche St, ending after a WS row.

Rep Rows 1–17 once more.

Work 5 rows even in Brioche St, ending after a WS row.

Break yarn. Place sts onto st holder or waste yarn.

back hem

Work as for Front Hem. Keep sts on needle. Do not break yarn.

body

Joining Row: (RS) Work in Brioche St to end of Back Hem sts, use the Backward Loop method (see Glossary) to CO 1 st, return 57 Front Hem sts to needles with RS facing, work in Brioche St to end, CO 1 st, pm for beg of rnd and join for working in rnds—116 sts.

Set-up Rnd: P1, [sl1yo, brp] 27 times, [sl1yo, p1] 2 times, [sl1yo, brp] 27 times, sl1yo, p1, sl1yo.

CONT CABLE PANEL

Rnd 1: [Sl1yo, brk] 5 times, sl1yo, *slm, [brk, sl1yo] 2 times, BR2/2RC, brk, BR2/2LC, [sl1yo, brk] 2 times, slm, work in Brioche St as est to next m; rep from * once more.

Rnds 2–8: Work 7 rnds even in Brioche St, ending after Rnd 2 of patt.

Rnd 9: Sl1yo, [brk, sl1yo] to m, *slm, brk, sl1yo, BR2/2RC, [brk, sl1yo] 2 times, brk, BR2/2LC, sl1yo, brk, slm, work in Brioche St as est to next m; rep from * once more.

Rnds 10–16: Work 7 rnds even in Brioche St, ending after Rnd 2 of patt.

Rnd 17: Sl1yo, [brk, sl1yo] to m, *slm, BR2/2RC, [brk, sl1yo] 4 times, brk, BR2/2LC, slm, work in Brioche St as est to next m; rep from * once more.

Rnds 18–24: Work 7 rnds even in Brioche St, ending after Rnd 2 of patt.

Rep last 24 rnds 2 more times.

Work 6 rnds in Brioche St, ending after Rnd 2 of patt.

BO loosely in patt as foll:

P1, brk, pass first st on RH needle over second st, binding off 1 st, *p1, pass first st on RH needle over second st, brk, pass first st on RH needle over second st; rep from * to end.

finishing

Weave in ends and lightly block to measurements. Because of the nature of Brioche St, steam blocking is advisable.

j o r a h

cardigan

Hebrew; casting forth

There is a beauty in simplicity of texture repeated. Jorah is worked from the bottom up, seamlessly, using simple brioche segments to create a cozy piece for daily wear. The yoke is shaped using simple decreases and the button band is a delicate accent. This is a great project for those who have recently mastered brioche and are looking to take their brioche knitting a step further.

Finished Sizes
34 (36½, 39½, 42, 45¼, 47½, 50¾, 55½, 58¾)" (86.5 [92.5, 100.5, 106.5, 115, 120.5, 129, 141, 149] cm) bust circumference, buttoned.

Designed to fit 31 (33, 36, 39, 42, 45, 48, 52, 56)" (78.5 [84, 91.5, 99, 106.5, 114.5, 122, 132, 142] cm) bust, with 2½–3½" (6.5–9 cm) added for ease.

Sweater shown measures 39½" (100.5 cm) and fits a 36" (91.5 cm) bust.

Yarn
Fingering weight (#2 Fine)

Shown here: Manos del Uruguay Milo (65% Merino wool, 35% linen; 380 yd

[350 m]/3½ oz [100 g]): #i7164 Amazonas, 4 (4, 4, 5, 5, 6, 6, 7, 7) hanks.

Needles
Size U.S. 5 (3.75 mm): 16" and 32" (40 and 80 cm) circular (cir).

Adjust needle size if necessary to obtain the correct gauge.

Notions
Stitch holders or waste yarn; yarn needle; 12 (12, 12, 12, 12, 13, 12, 12, 12) buttons to fit buttonholes (see photo on page 116).

Gauge
20 sts = 4" (10 cm) and 4, 14-row repeats (56 rows) = 4½" (11.5 cm) in Brioche Segment Patt, worked flat.

(When counting the 14-row repeats of the Brioche Segment Patt, note that each 14-row repeat looks like only 8 rows. So 4, 14-row repeats would look like 32 rows.)

Notes
⟶ Because this piece is worked seamlessly from the bottom up, there is minimal finishing.

⟶ Instructions are provided for binding off the neckband, but you may substitute another elastic bind-off.

⟶ Circular needles are recommended to accommodate large number of sts. Do not join; work back and forth in rows.

Stitch Guide

1×1 RIBBING (MULTIPLE OF 2 STS + 1)

Row 1: (WS) K1, *p1, k1; rep from * to end.

Row 2: K2, *p1, k1; rep from * to last st, k1.

Rep Rows 1 and 2 for patt.

BRIOCHE SEGMENT PATT (MULTIPLE OF 2 STS + 1)

Row 1: (RS) K1, *k1, sl1yo; rep from * to last 2 sts, k2.

Row 2: K1, *sl1yo, brk; rep from * to last 2 sts, sl1yo, k1.

Row 3: K1, *brk, sl1yo; rep from * to last 2 sts, brk, k1.

Rows 4–11: Rep Rows 2 and 3.

Row 12: Rep Row 2.

Row 13: *K1, brk; rep from * to last st, k1.

Row 14: K1, purl to last st, k1.

Rep Rows 1–14 for patt.

CHAIN 4
*Slip the st on the RH needle onto the LH needle and knit into it; rep from * 3 more times.

body

Using longer needles, CO 187 (197, 213, 227, 243, 257, 273, 293, 313) sts. Do not join; work back and forth in rows.

Work in 1×1 Ribbing (see Stitch Guide) until piece meas 1" (2.5 cm) from CO edge, ending after a WS row.

Next Row: (RS) Knit.

Next Row: (WS) K1, purl to last st, k1.

BEGIN BRIOCHE SEGMENT PATT

Work Rows 1–14 of Brioche Segment Patt (see Stitch Guide) 10 (10, 10, 10, 10, 11, 11, 11, 11) times, then rep Rows 1–12 once more.

Set aside, keeping sts on longer cir needle and yarn attached to body.

sleeves (make 2)

Using shorter cir needle, CO 49 (51, 53, 55, 55, 57, 57, 59, 59) sts. Do not join; work back and forth in rows.

Work in 1×1 Ribbing until piece meas 1 (1, 1, 1½, 1½, 1½, 1½, 1½, 1½)" (2.5 [2.5, 2.5, 3.8, 3.8, 3.8, 3.8, 3.8, 3.8] cm) from CO edge, ending after a WS row.

Next Row: (RS) Knit.

Next Row: K1, purl to last st, k1.

BEGIN BRIOCHE SEGMENT PATT AND SHAPE SLEEVE

Rows 1–12: Work Rows 1–12 of Brioche Segment Patt.

Row 13, Inc Row: (RS) K1, brk, kfb, *brk, k1; rep from * to last 4 sts, brk, kfb, brk, k1—2 sts inc'd.

Row 14, Inc Row: (WS) K1, p5, pfb, purl to last 7 sts, pfb, p5, k1—2 sts inc'd.

Rep last 14 rows 0 (0, 1, 1, 1, 3, 4, 5, 6) more time(s)—53 (55, 61, 63, 63, 73, 77, 83, 87) sts.

Cont working Rows 1–14 of Brioche Segment Patt, without inc further, 9 (9, 9, 8, 7, 5, 4, 3, 2) more times, then rep Rows 1–12 once more.

Place the first and last 4 sts onto a st holder or waste yarn for under-arm. Break yarn. Place rem 45 (47, 53, 55, 55, 65, 69, 75, 79) sts onto a separate st holder or waste yarn.

yoke

JOIN SLEEVES TO BODY

Cont using longer cir needle and yarn attached to body.

Joining Row: (RS) K43 (45, 49, 53, 57, 61, 65, 69, 75) sts across Body, place next 8 Body sts onto st holder or waste yarn for underarm, return 45 (47, 53, 55, 55, 65, 69, 75, 79) held Sleeve sts to needle and knit across, k85 (91, 99, 105, 113, 119, 127, 139, 147) Body sts for back, place next 8 Body sts onto st holder or waste yarn for underarm, return 45 (47, 53, 55, 55, 65, 69, 75, 79) held Sleeve sts to needle and knit across, knit to end of Body—261 (275, 303, 321, 337, 369, 395, 425, 453) sts.

Next Row: (WS) K1, purl to last st, k1.

Work Rows 1–14 of Brioche Segment Patt 1 (1, 1, 1, 1, 2, 2, 2, 2) time(s), then rep Rows 1–13 once more.

Dec Row 1: (RS) K4 (3, 5, 1, 1, 3, 3, 3, 2), *k2tog, k2; rep from * to last 1 (0, 2, 0, 0, 0, 0, 0, 1) st(s), knit to end—197 (207, 229, 241, 253, 279, 297, 321, 342) sts rem.

Work Rows 1–14 of Brioche Segment Patt 1 (1, 1, 1, 1, 1, 1, 2, 2) more time(s), then rep Rows 1–13 once more.

Dec Row 2: (RS) K3 (2, 1, 1, 1, 2, 2, 2, 3), *k2tog, k1; rep from * to last 2 (1, 0, 0, 0, 1, 1, 1, 0) st(s), knit to end—133 (139, 153, 161, 169, 187, 199, 215, 229) sts rem.

Rep Rows 1–13 of Brioche Segment Patt:

Work for your selected size as foll:

Sizes 34 (36½, 39½, 47½, 50¾)"
(86.5 [92.5, 100.5, 120.5, 129] cm) Only
Dec Row 3: (RS) [K1, k2tog] 3 (4, 3, 2, 4) times, [k2tog, k1, k2tog] 23 (23, 27, 35, 35) times, [k2tog, k1] 3 (4, 3, 2, 4) times—81 (85, 93, 113, 121) sts rem.

The top two buttons are shaped like fox heads and more closely spaced than the rest of the buttons, which are round.

Sizes 42 and 45¼" (106.5 and 115 cm) Only
Dec Row 3: (RS) *K1 (2), [k2tog] 2 times; rep from * to last 1 (2) st(s), knit to end—97 (103) sts rem.

Size 55½" (141 cm) Only
Dec Row 3: (RS) *K2tog, k1, k2tog; rep from * to end—129 sts rem.

Size 58¾" (149 cm) Only
Dec Row 3: (RS) *[K2tog] 2 times, k1; rep from * to last 4 sts, [k2tog] 2 times—137 sts rem.

All Sizes

Work 4 (6, 8, 10, 12, 12, 12, 2, 2) rows in Brioche Segment Patt as est, then work Row 13 once.

Work for your selected size as foll:

Sizes 34 (42, 45¼, 55½)" (86.5 [106.5, 115, 141] cm) Only
Dec Row 4: (RS) *K10 (12, 13, 8), k2tog; rep from * to last 9 (13, 13, 9) sts, knit to end—75 (91, 97, 117) sts rem.

Sizes 36½ (39½, 47½, 50¾, 58¾)"
(92.5 [100.5, 120.5, 129, 149] cm) Only
Dec Row 4: (RS) K12 (7, 11, 10, 7), [k2tog, k10 (9, 8, 7, 9)] 5 (7, 9, 11, 11) times, k2tog, knit to end—79 (85, 103, 109, 125) sts rem.

NECKBAND

Work in 1×1 Ribbing until ribbing meas 1" (2.5 cm) ending after a WS row.

BO all sts using 1×1 Elastic Bind-off (see Glossary).

left button band

With RS facing and shorter cir needle, pick up and knit 137 (139, 139, 141, 143, 153, 155, 157, 159) sts along left front selvedge edge working from neckband to hem. Do not join; work back and forth in rows.

Knit 5 rows.

BO all sts loosely.

right button band

With RS facing and shorter cir needle, pick up and knit 137 (139, 139, 141, 143, 153, 155, 157, 159) sts along left front selvedge edge working from hem to neckband. Do not join; work back and forth in rows.

Next Row: (WS) Knit.

Next Row: (RS) BO 1 (2, 2, 3, 5, 3, 0, 1, 2), chain 4 (see Stitch Guide), [BO 13 (13, 13, 13, 13, 13, 15, 15, 15), chain 4] 10 (10, 10, 10, 10, 11, 10, 10, 10) times, BO 5, chain 4, BO 1 (2, 2, 3, 3, 2, 0, 1, 2). Break yarn.

finishing

Starting at the cuff, seam the sleeves closed. Graft sleeve underarm and body underarm together.

Weave in ends and block to measurements.

Sew buttons to Left Button Band, lining them up with the corresponding buttonholes on the Right Button Band.

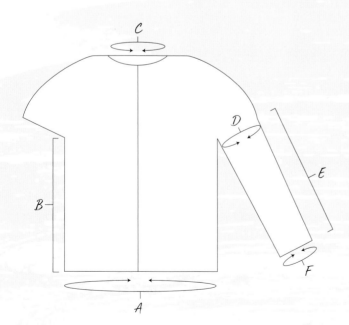

A: 34 (36½, 39½, 42, 45¼, 47½, 50¾, 55½, 58¾)" 86.5 [92.5, 100.5, 106.5, 115, 120.5, 129, 141, 149] cm)

B: 13½ (13½, 13½, 13½, 13½, 14½, 14½, 14½, 14½)" 34.5 [34.5, 34.5, 34.5, 34.5, 37, 37, 37, 37] cm)

C: 15 (15¾, 17, 18¼, 19½, 20½, 21¾, 23½, 25)" 38 [40, 43, 46.5, 49.5, 52, 55, 59.5, 63.5] cm)

D: 10½ (11, 12¼, 12½, 12½, 14½, 15½, 16½, 17½)" 26.5 [28, 31, 32, 32, 37, 39.5, 42, 44.5] cm)

E: 12¾ (12¾, 13¾, 13¼, 12¼, 12¼, 12½, 12½, 12½)" 32.5 [32.5, 35, 33.5, 31, 31, 32, 32, 32] cm

F: 9¾ (10¼, 10½, 11, 11, 11½, 11½, 11¾, 11¾)" 25 [26, 26.5, 28, 28, 29, 29, 30, 30] cm)

chapter five

All Heaven and Earth
Flowered white obliterate . . .
Snow . . . unceasing snow

— BASHO MATSUO

Winter

ALL-OVER CABLE & COLOR

Though many of us think of winter as a time to dig into knitting gifts for the holidays, it's also the perfect time to stitch up some heavier pieces for ourselves that can be worn on truly frigid days. Just as the cold blue morning light begins to filter through the trees, I'm outside breaking ice, tossing corn, and packing straw into the henhouse. My kitchen floor begins to gather piles of woolen stoles and sweaters, shed with a layer of freshly accumulated snow on the shoulders. I simply can't leave the house without at least one large wool piece on my back. The winter garments in this chapter are made for the cold. Each features either all-over color or cables that add warmth to the fabric.

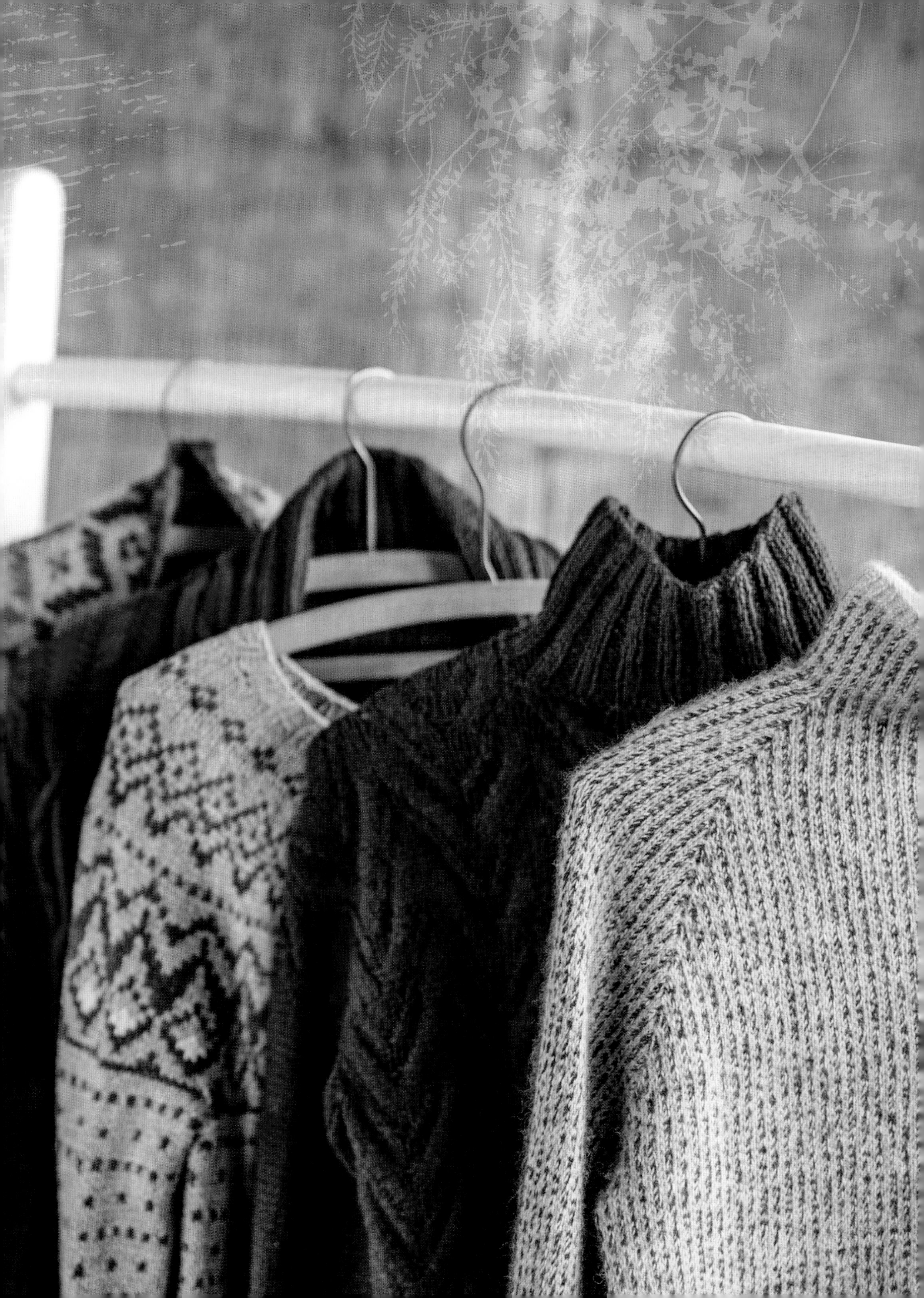

l u m i
sweater

Finnish; snowy weather

Worked from the bottom up in rounds, in a gauge that knits up quickly, and incorporating a deceptively simple cable pattern, Lumi can be made fast. I love a tidy pullover for the cold months when I know I'll be throwing my coat on every few hours—something that isn't fussy when layering. The shoulder shaping creates a sweeping drop-sleeve style without adding a lot of baggy fabric. Lumi is designed to be slightly cropped, but instructions for lengthening are included.

Finished Sizes

33 (36, 39, 42, 45, 48, 51, 54)" (84 [91.5, 99, 106.5, 114.5, 122, 129.5, 137] cm) bust circumference.

Designed to fit 32 (35, 38, 41, 44, 47, 50, 53)" (81.5 [89, 96.5, 104, 112, 119.5, 127, 134.5] cm) bust, with 1" (2.5 cm) added for ease.

Sweater shown measures 36" (91.5 cm) and fits a 35" (89 cm) bust.

Yarn

Worsted weight (#4 Medium).

Shown here: Blue Sky Fibers Woolstock (100% Highland wool; 123 yd [113 m]/1¾ oz [50 g]): #1314 Deep Velvet, 8 (9, 10, 10, 11, 12, 12, 13) hanks.

> **Note:** Increasing the body length requires at least one additional hank of yarn.

Needles

Size U.S. 7 (4.5 mm): 16" and 32" (40 cm and 80 cm) circular (cir) and set of 4 or 5 double-pointed (dpn).

Adjust needle size if necessary to obtain the correct gauge.

Notions

Markers (m); cable needle (cn); stitch holders or waste yarn; yarn needle.

Gauge

22 sts and 25 rnds = 4" (10 cm) in St st worked in rnds.

16 sts (1 stitch repeat) = 3" (7.5 cm) and 28 rnds (2 row repeats) = 3¾" (9.5 cm) in cable patt worked in rnds.

Notes

⌐ Body is worked from the bottom up in rounds, top front and back are worked flat and joined at the shoulders before sleeves are picked up and knit from the armholes and worked in rounds to the cuff.

Stitch Guide

2×2 RIBBING (MULTIPLE OF 4 STS)

Rnd 1: K1, *p2, k2; rep from * to last 3 sts, p2, k1.

Rep Rnd 1 for patt.

body

Using longer cir needle, CO 176 (192, 208, 224, 240, 256, 272, 288) sts. Pm for beg of rnd and join for working in rnds, being careful not to twist sts.

Begin Cable Chart, working Rnds 1–19 once, then rep Rnds 20–33 until piece meas 10¾ (11¼, 11½, 11½, 11½, 11½, 11½, 11½)" (27.5 [28.5, 29, 29, 29, 29, 29, 29] cm) or preferred length from CO edge, ending after an even rnd.

> *Note: This pullover is designed to be worn cropped; if you prefer a longer sweater, work to the preferred length from hem to underarm.*

DIVIDE FRONT AND BACK

Next Rnd: Work in patt as est over next 88 (96, 104, 112, 120, 128, 136, 144) sts for Front, transfer rem 88 (96, 104, 112, 120, 128, 136, 144) sts onto st holder or waste yarn for Back. Cont working back and forth over Front sts only.

front

SHAPE ARMHOLES

Row 1, Inc Row: (WS) K1, M1, purl to last st, M1, k1—2 sts inc'd.

Row 2: (RS) K1, work in patt as est to last st, k1.

Row 3: K1, purl to last st, k1.

Row 4: Rep Row 2.

Rep last 4 rows 9 (9, 9, 10, 10, 11, 11, 11) more times—108 (116, 124, 134, 142, 152, 160, 168) sts.

Sizes 33 (48)" (84 [122] cm) Only

Rep Row 3 once more.

Sizes 36 (42, 51, 54)" (91.5 [106.5, 129.5, 137] cm) Only

Rep Row 1 once more—118 (136, 162, 170) sts.

Sizes 39 (45)" (99 [114.5] cm) Only

Rep Rows 1–3 once more—126 (144) sts.

SHAPE SHOULDERS

Row 1: (RS) BO 8 (9, 10, 12, 12, 13, 14, 15) sts, work in patt as est to end.

Row 2: (WS) BO 8 (9, 10, 12, 12, 13, 14, 15) sts, purl to end.

Rep last 2 rows 2 more times—60 (64, 66, 64, 72, 74, 78, 80) sts rem.

Next Row: (RS) BO 2 sts, work in patt as est over next 14 (14, 14, 13, 15, 15, 16, 16) sts, place next 28 (32, 34, 34, 38, 40, 42, 44) onto holder for front neck, place last 16 (16, 16, 15, 17, 17, 18, 18) sts onto st holder or waste yarn for Right Shoulder. Cont working over Left Shoulder sts only.

Left Shoulder

Row 1: (WS) Purl.

Row 2: (RS) BO 2 sts, work in patt as est to end.

Rep last 2 rows once, then rep Row 1 once more—10 (10, 10, 9, 11, 11, 12, 12) sts rem.

Next Row: (RS) BO all Left Shoulder sts.

CABLE CHART

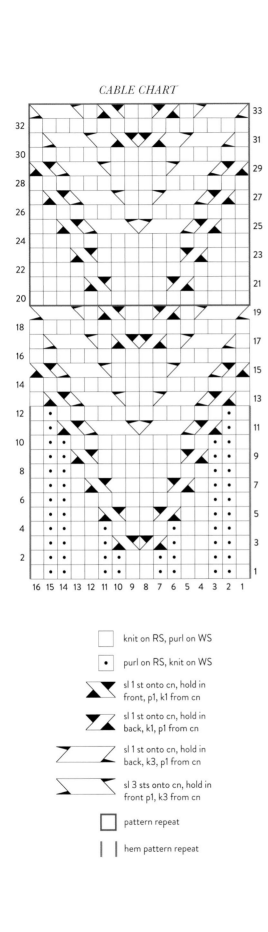

knit on RS, purl on WS

• purl on RS, knit on WS

sl 1 st onto cn, hold in
front, p1, k1 from cn

sl 1 st onto cn, hold in
back, k1, p1 from cn

sl 1 st onto cn, hold in
back, k3, p1 from cn

sl 3 sts onto cn, hold in
front p1, k3 from cn

pattern repeat

hem pattern repeat

Right Shoulder

Return 16 (16, 16, 15, 17, 17, 18, 18) held Right Shoulder sts to needle and rejoin yarn with RS facing.

Row 1: (RS) Work in patt as est to end.

Row 2: BO 2 sts, purl to end.

Rep last 2 rows 2 more times, then rep Row 1 once more—10 (10, 10, 9, 11, 11, 12, 12) sts rem.

Next Row: (WS) BO all Right Shoulder sts.

back

Return 88 (96, 104, 112, 120, 128, 136, 144) held Back sts to needles and rejoin yarn with RS facing.

Next Row: (RS) Work in patt as est to end.

SHAPE ARMHOLES

Work same as Front—108 (118, 126, 136, 144, 152, 162, 170) sts rem.

SHAPE SHOULDERS

Row 1: (RS) BO 8 (9, 10, 12, 12, 13, 14, 15) sts, work in patt as est to end.

Row 2: (WS) BO 8 (9, 10, 12, 12, 13, 14, 15) sts, purl to end.

Rows 3–6: Rep last 2 rows 2 more times—60 (64, 66, 64, 72, 74, 78, 80) sts rem.

Row 7: BO 2 sts, work in patt as est to end.

Row 8: BO 2 sts, purl to end.

Rows 9–12: Rep last 2 rows 2 more times—48 (52, 54, 52, 60, 62, 66, 68) sts rem.

Row 13: BO 10 (10, 10, 9, 11, 11, 12, 12) sts, work in patt as est to end.

Row 14: BO 10 (10, 10, 9, 11, 11, 12, 12) sts—28 (32, 34, 34, 38, 40, 42, 44) sts rem.

Place rem sts onto st holder or waste yarn for neck.

Break yarn.

sleeves

Using dpns, pick up and knit 64 (68, 70, 74, 76, 76, 80, 80) sts around armhole. Pm for beg of rnd and join for working in rnds.

SHAPE SLEEVE

Knit 5 (4, 4, 4, 3, 4, 3, 3) rnds.

Dec Rnd: K1, ssk, knit to last 3 sts, k2tog, k1—2 sts dec'd.

Rep last 6 (5, 5, 5, 4, 5, 4, 4) rnds 12 (13, 14, 15, 16, 15, 17, 16) more times—38 (40, 40, 42, 42, 44, 44, 46) sts rem.

Work even in St st until sleeve meas 12¾ (13, 13, 13¼, 13¼, 13¼, 13¼, 13½)" (32.5 [33, 33, 33.5, 33.5, 33.5, 33.5, 34.5] cm) from underarm.

Next Rnd: *K1, p1; rep from * to end.

Rep last rnd until cuff meas 1½" (4 cm). BO all sts in patt.

finishing

Seam Front and Back Shoulders together.

NECKBAND

Using shorter needles and with RS facing, beg at Left Shoulder seam, pick up and knit 6 (8, 6, 6, 10, 8, 6, 12) sts along left neckline, k28 (32, 34, 34, 38, 40, 42, 44) held Front sts, pick up and knit 6 (8, 6, 6, 10, 8, 6, 12) sts along right neckline to Right Shoulder seam, k28 (32, 34, 34, 38, 40, 42, 44) held Back sts, pm for beg of rnd and join for working in rnds—68 (80, 80, 80, 96, 96, 96, 112) sts.

Purl 1 rnd.

Work 2x2 Ribbing (see Stitch Guide) for 4" (10 cm).

BO all sts in patt.

Weave in ends and block to measurements.

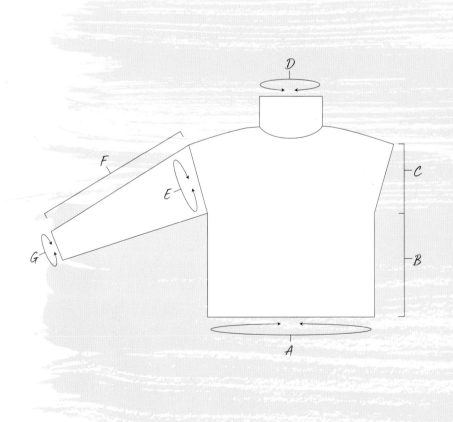

A: 33 (36, 39, 42, 45, 48, 51, 54)"
84 [91.5, 99, 106.5, 114.5, 122, 129.5, 137] cm)

B: 10¾ (11¼, 11½, 11½, 11½, 11½, 11½, 11½)"
27.5 [28.5, 29, 29, 29, 29, 29, 29] cm)

C: 5½ (5½, 5¾, 6, 6¼, 6½, 6½, 6½)"
14 [14, 14.5, 15, 16, 16.5, 16.5, 16.5] cm)

D: 12¼ (14½, 14½, 14½, 17½, 17½, 17½, 20¼)"
31 [37, 37, 37, 44.5, 44.5, 44.5, 51.5] cm)

E: 11¾ (12¼, 12¾, 13½, 13¾, 13¾, 14½, 14½)"
30 [31, 32.5, 34.5, 35, 35, 37, 37] cm)

F: 14¼ (14½, 14½, 14¾, 14¾, 14¾, 14¾, 15)"
36 [37, 37, 37.5, 37.5, 37.5, 37.5, 38] cm)

G: 7 (7¼, 7¼, 7¾, 7¾, 8, 8, 8¼)"
18 [18.5, 18.5, 19.5, 19.5, 20.5, 20.5, 21] cm)

quilo
cape

Greek; North wind

I originally wanted to include a circular blanket/shawl in this collection, but as I started thinking about how little I wear my circular and semicircular shawls, I decided to put on my thinking cap and come up with a shape that could be worked in rounds, show off some great shaping, and still be long enough to wrap up in. The oval-shaped Quilo was born. This large, heavy stole combines classic colorwork and contemporary shaping to create a truly unique accessory for cold winter months. Color stranding provides an extra layer of wool that boosts the stole's warmth while showcasing the oval construction.

Finished Size
56½" (143.5 cm) wide and 27¼" (69 cm) across the center.

Yarn
Worsted weight (#4 Medium).

Shown here: Elsa Wool Woolen Spun Worsted (100% Cormo wool; 237 yd [217 m]/4 oz [115 g]): #3384 (A), 1 hank; #3385 (B), 2 hanks; #3395 (C), 2 hanks; #3399 (D), 1 hank.

Needles
Size U.S. 8 (5 mm): 60" (152 cm) circular (cir).

Adjust needle size if necessary to obtain the correct gauge.

Notions
Markers (m); removable markers; yarn needle.

Gauge
18 sts and 22 rnds = 4" (10 cm) in St st worked in rnds.

Notes
⌐ This piece is worked simply in rounds and seamed along the center to close the stole and create the oval shape.

⌐ All colorwork is charted with stitch counts listed on increase rounds; work repeats within red box as shown in chart key.

Stitch Guide

LEFT LIFTED INCREASE (LLI)

K1, insert LH needle into the left leg of the st below the new st on the RH needle, knit through the back of the lifted leg—1 st inc'd.

INVISIBLE SEAM

With the cast-on edges together and lined up stitch for stitch, insert tapestry needle under both legs of the first stitch along the edge of the bottom row, then under both legs of the first stitch along the edge of the top row; rep from *, alternating bottom and top rows until all stitches are seamed.

body

Using color A, CO 280 sts. Place contrasting m for beg of rnd and join for working in rnds, being careful not to twist sts.

Set-up Rnd: *K4, pm, k132, pm, k8, pm, k132, pm, k4.

After working the next rnd, place removable markers on the CO edge to mark the marker placement in the Set-up Rnd. These will be used in finishing.

Work Rnds 1–75 of Chart, working inc rnds 3, 9, 21, and 46 as foll:

Inc Rnd: [K1, LLI] to m, slm, *knit to m, slm, [K1, LLI] to m; rep from * to end.

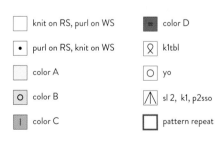

knit on RS, purl on WS	≈ color D
• purl on RS, knit on WS	♀ k1tbl
color A	O yo
○ color B	⋀ sl 2, k1, p2sso
I color C	☐ pattern repeat

Chart row numbers (right side, top to bottom): 75, 74, 73, 72, 71, 70, 69, 68, 67, 66, 65, 64, 63, 62, 61, 60, 59, 58, 57, 56, 55, 54, 53, 52, 51, 50, 49, 48, 47, inc rnd-520 sts, 45, 44, 43, 42, 41, 40, 39, 38, 37, 36, 35, 34, 33, 32, 31, 30, 29, 28, 27, 26, 25, 24, 23, 22, inc rnd-392 sts, 20, 19, 18, 17, 16, 15, 14, 13, 12, 11, 10, inc rnd-328 sts, 8, 7, 6, 5, 4, inc rnd-296 sts, 2, 1

Chart column numbers (bottom): 20 19 18 17 16 15 14 13 12 11 10 9 8 7 6 5 4 3 2 1

border

Bobble Rnd: Using color D, BO 4 sts in patt, *k1, yo, k1 into next st, turn, p1, p1tbl, p1, turn, k3, turn, p3, turn, k3, [pass second st on RH needle over first] 3 times, BO 9 sts in patt; rep from * to end. All sts are bound off.

finishing

With RS facing, position the CO edges for the body of the stole horizontally with a top row and a bottom row with marked sts on each end. Using color A, start with the 8 sts to the right of the markers on the right end of the stole. Insert tapestry needle into each CO edge of the 8 sts and pull tight. Starting with the next st on the bottom row and top row respectively to the left of the markers, seam the CO edge closed using the invisible seam (see Stitch Guide) until reaching the markers on the left end of the stole. Insert tapestry needle into each CO edge of the 8 sts to the left of the markers and pull tight.

Weave in ends and block to measurements.

The border features evenly spaced bobbles.

elsawool

I loved working with the soft, undyed, lanolin-rich yarn from Elsawool. I'm not ashamed to say I'm a professional yarn sniffer, and I spent as much time huffing the earthy perfume of this yarn as I did cuddling and knitting with it. I knew instantly that I needed to reach out to Elsa to learn a bit more about her company and her fiber journey, one that began more than thirty years ago.

Animals have been central to Elsa's life since the 1940s. She grew up surrounded by farm animals, managed a pet farm, and worked at an animal hospital, among other things. Art and various crafts have also been a big part of her life. Eventually Elsa's love of animals and her interest in making beautiful things converged into a fascination with fiber animals. She started breeding sheep and Angora goats in 1983, with the goal of producing high-quality animal fiber in black, gray, brown, red, and other colors. Eventually, wanting better fleece quality, she sought out Cormo sheep.

After putting her hands into their fine, uniform, deep, dense, and extremely soft fleeces, Elsa knew she'd found her breed. All the Cormos she located were white, but the breed was developed from Corriedale and superfine Merino stock, many of which carry recessive genes for black wool, so Elsa believed that white Cormos could produce black and gray offspring. She sold all her other fiber animals, and had soon purchased 200 or so beautiful white Cormo sheep. Every year, she selected for dark hooves, dark eyelids, and dark noses, along with sound conformation, good wool, and good temperament. In the early 1990s, one of the ewes produced a black lamb. The next

year another ewe had a black lamb. Eventually a third of the flock consisted of black and gray sheep. For about thirty years, this Cormo flock produced exceptionally good white, black, and gray wool.

Elsa now buys top-quality white, black, and gray Cormo wool from a family in Montana. The wool is washed in Texas, sent to woolen and worsted spinning mills in other states, and spun into different types of yarns. Some of the yarns are sold to hand-knitters, others are knitted into clothing, but all of the yarns and pieces of clothing are designed to highlight the softness and elasticity of Cormo wool.

WHY WOOLEN SPUN WORSTED?

The yarn used for Quilo is blended wools from Cormo sheep with different natural coloring in a worsted weight that works up quickly for a piece of this size. The range of shades available from Elsa's sheep is impressive, to say the least, from creamy white to bitter chocolate black, with every warm gray in between. The lofty woolen-spun wool is a cocoon of soft-to-the-skin warmth, and the company has deep roots in the USA from start to finish.

Once the giant Quilo shawl was off the needles, blocked, and dry, I flung it around my shoulders and made my way out to close the henhouse with temperatures deep in the negatives and iced-over snow crunching underfoot. I knew it was going to be difficult to give Quilo up for even the short time it would take to have it photographed for this book.

neve

colorwork pullover

Italian; Snow

This classic pullover features top-down construction and the ever-popular circular yoke. With minimal shaping and a larger gauge, this sweater is a whip to make for experienced knitters, but its short-rows and colorwork shouldn't deter advanced beginners looking to learn new skills. The top-down construction is a friendly approach for those who dislike knitting sleeves from the cuff up. Color gives an opportunity to play with contrast and hue, unlocking the unique creativity in every knitter.

Finished Sizes

35¼ (38¾, 40½, 42, 47¼, 48¾, 52¼, 55½, 57¼)" (89.5 [98.5, 103, 106.5, 120, 124, 132.5, 141, 145.5] cm) bust circumference.

Designed to fit 30¼ (33¾, 35½, 37, 42¼, 43¾, 47¼, 50½, 52¼)" (77 [85.5, 90, 94, 107.5, 111, 120, 128.5, 132.5] cm) bust, with 5" (12.5 cm) added for ease.

Sweater shown measures 40½" (103 cm) and fits a 35½" (90 cm) bust.

Yarn

Worsted weight (#4 Medium).

Shown here: O-Wool Balance (50% organic cotton, 50% organic Merino wool; 130 yd [120 m]/1¾ oz [50 g]): Jade (light green, A), 5 (5, 6, 6, 7, 7, 8, 8, 9) hanks; Emerald (dark green, B), 2 (2, 2, 3, 3, 3, 4, 4, 4) hanks; Desert Blush (pink, C), 1 (1, 1, 1, 2, 2, 2, 2, 3) hank(s).

Needles

Size U.S. 7 (4.5 mm): 16" and 32" (40 and 80 cm) circular (cir) and set of 4 or 5 double-pointed (dpn).

Adjust needle size if necessary to obtain the correct gauge.

Notions

Markers (m); stitch holders or waste yarn; yarn needle.

Gauge

19 sts and 25 rnds = 4" (10 cm) in St st worked in rnds.

Notes

⁓ When working stranded colorwork, make sure there's plenty of space between stitches on the needle so that the fabric will maintain stretch. Longer floats can be secured by picking up the float and knitting it with a centrally placed stitch on the following round.

1×1 RIBBING (MULTIPLE OF 2 STS)

Rnd 1: *K1, p1; rep from * to end.

Rep Rnd 1 for patt.

yoke

Using color A and shorter cir needles, CO 64 (68, 76, 80, 84, 92, 96, 104, 108) sts. Pm for beg of rnd and join for working in rnds, being careful not to twist sts.

Work even in 1×1 Ribbing (see Stitch Guide) until piece meas 1" (2.5 cm) from CO edge.

Short-row 1: (RS) K6 (7, 7, 8, 8, 9, 9, 10, 10), turn.

Short-row 2: Sl1, p11 (13, 13, 15, 15, 17, 17, 19, 19), turn.

Short-row 3: Sl1, knit to 1 st before gap, close gap (see Glossary), k6 (7, 7, 8, 8, 9, 9, 10, 10), turn.

Short-row 4: Sl1, purl to 1 st before gap, close gap, p6 (7, 7, 8, 8, 9, 9, 10, 10), turn.

Rep Short-rows 3 and 4 once more.

Next Row: (RS) Sl1, knit to end. Do not turn; cont working in the rnd.

Next Rnd: Knit to end, closing rem gaps.

Knit 0 (0, 1, 1, 2, 2, 3, 3, 5) rnd(s).

BEGIN CHARTS & SHAPE YOKE

Change to longer cir needle as needed.

Work Rnds 1–16 of Chart 1, increasing and joining color B as indicated—128 (136, 152, 160, 168, 184, 192, 208, 216) sts after Rnd 1 Inc; 192 (204, 228, 240, 252, 276, 288, 312, 324) sts after Rnd 5 Inc.

Using color A, knit 1 (2, 2, 3, 3, 4, 4, 5, 5) rnd(s) even.

Sizes 35¼ (40½, 42, 47¼, 48¾, 52¼, 55½, 57¼)"
(89.5 [103, 106.5, 120, 124, 132.5, 141, 145.5] cm) Only
Inc Rnd: K2, [M1, k3 (5, 5, 3, 3, 3, 3, 3)] 16 (10, 8, 26, 14, 32, 20, 22) times, [M1, k4] 23 (31, 39, 23, 47, 23, 47, 47) times, [M1, k3 (5, 5, 3, 3, 3, 3, 3)] to last 2 sts, M1, k2—248 (280, 296, 328, 352, 376, 400, 416) sts.

Size 38¾" (98.5 cm) Only
Inc Rnd: K1, [M1, k3] to last 2 sts, M1, k2—272 sts.

All Sizes
Work Rnds 1–21 of Chart 2, joining color C as indicated.

BREAK FOR SLEEVES

Using color B, k40 (44, 46, 48, 54, 56, 60, 64, 66), k44 (48, 48, 52, 56, 64, 68, 72, 76) and place onto st holder or waste yarn for right sleeve, k80 (88, 92, 96, 108, 112, 120, 128, 132) for Front, k44 (48, 48, 52, 56, 64, 68, 72, 76) and place onto st holder or waste yarn for left sleeve, knit to end—80 (88, 92, 96, 108, 112, 120, 128, 132) sts rem each Front and Back.

body

Using color A, knit to held sts for right sleeve, CO2, pm, CO2, knit to held sts for left sleeve, CO2, pm, CO2, knit to end—168 (184, 192, 200, 224, 232, 248, 264, 272) sts. Or, instead of doing this, you could try the Double Underarm Cast-on method. See sidebar at far right to learn how.

Work Rnds 2–8 of Chart 3, then rep Rnds 1–8, 5 (5, 6, 6, 6, 6, 6, 6, 6) more times.

Work Rnds 9–22 once, then rep Rnd 22 nine more times.

BO all sts loosely in patt.

CHART 1

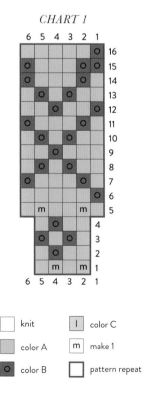

CHART 2

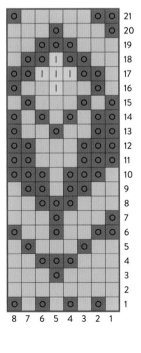

	knit
	color A
	color B

I	color C
m	make 1
	pattern repeat

DOUBLE UNDERARM CAST-ON

If you're feeling adventurous, try my Double Underarm Cast-on and avoid picking up stitches later. It's a bit tricky at first, but a fun addition to your knitting skill set. Here's how it's done:

Turn the work so WS is facing. Purl into the first st, leaving it on the LH needle, and place the new st from the RH needle onto the LH needle, essentially casting on as for a knitted cast-on, but purlwise. Repeat the action, casting on 8 sts.

Then, carefully transfer the first, third, fifth, and seventh CO sts to a stitch holder and return the second, fourth, sixth, and eighth CO sts to the LH needle. Turn work so that RS is facing and continue knitting across the sweater body. The held sts will become the underarm stitches when working the sleeves.

CHART 3

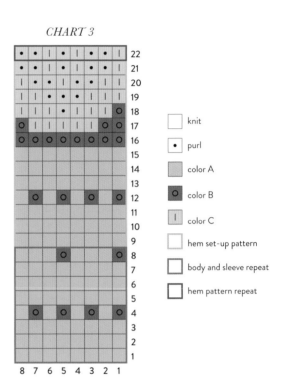

☐	knit
•	purl
▨	color A
⊙	color B
▏	color C
☐	hem set-up pattern
☐	body and sleeve repeat
☐	hem pattern repeat

sleeves

With RS facing, color A and dpns, beg at marker for center underarm, pick up and knit 2 sts, k44 (48, 48, 52, 56, 64, 68, 72, 76) held sts, pick up and knit 2 sts—48 (52, 52, 56, 60, 68, 72, 76, 80) sts. Pm for beg of rnd and join to work in rnds.

> **Note:** *If using the Double Underarm Cast-on described on the previous page, rather than picking up and knitting, simply knit the 2 cast-on sts starting at the center underarm, then knit the last 2 cast-on sts at the end of the rnd.*

BEGIN CHART 3

Read the following instructions carefully before beginning. The sleeve shaping begins at the same time as Chart 3.

Work Rnds 2–8 of Chart 3, rep Rnds 1–8 ten times, then work Rnds 9–22 once.

SHAPE SLEEVE

Work in patt for 19 (13, 13, 10, 7, 6, 6, 5, 4) rnds.

Dec Rnd: K1, k2tog, work in patt to last 3 sts, ssk, k1—2 sts dec'd.

Rep last 20 (14, 14, 11, 8, 7, 7, 6, 5) rnds 3 (5, 5, 7, 9, 11, 11, 13, 15) more times—40 (40, 40, 40, 40, 40, 48, 48, 48) sts rem.

Cont working Chart 3 as est until Rnds 9–22 are completed once, then rep Rnd 22 nine more times.

BO all sts loosely in patt.

finishing

Weave in ends and block to measurements.

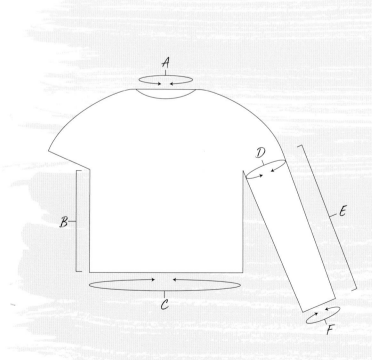

A: 13½ (14¼, 16, 16¾, 17¾, 19¼, 20¼, 22, 22¾)"
34.5 [36, 40.5, 42.5, 45, 49, 51.5, 56, 58] cm)

B: 11¼ (11¼, 12¾, 12¾, 12¾, 12¾, 12¾, 12¾, 12¾)"
28.5 [28.5, 32.5, 32.5, 32.5, 32.5, 32.5, 32.5, 32.5] cm)

C: 35¼ (38¾, 40½, 42, 47¼, 48¾, 52¼, 55½, 57¼)"
89.5 [98.5, 103, 106.5, 120, 124, 132.5, 141, 145.5] cm)

D: 10 (11, 11, 11¾, 12¾, 14¼, 15¼, 16, 16¾)"
25.5 [28, 28, 30, 32.5, 36, 38.5, 40.5, 42.5] cm)

E: 16½" (42 cm)

F: 8½ (8½, 8½, 8½, 8½, 9¼, 10, 10, 10)"
21.5 [21.5, 21.5, 21.5, 21.5, 23.5, 25.5, 25.5, 25.5] cm)

eira

cardigan

Welsh; snow

The casual fit of this cardigan makes it an instant classic, perfect for layering in the cold months. It's worked flat from the bottom up in pieces, with multiple cable motifs worked at once and a simple front band with a closure. The real beauty of Eira, though, is in the traveling yoke and oversized neck.

Finished Sizes

34 (37½, 39½, 43, 45½, 49, 51½, 53½, 57, 59½)" (86.5 [95.5, 100.5, 109, 115.5, 124.5, 131, 136, 145, 151] cm) bust circumference.

Designed to fit 30½ (34, 36, 39½, 42, 45½, 48, 50, 53½, 56)" (77.5 [86.5, 91.5, 100.5, 106.5, 115.5, 122, 127, 136, 142] cm) bust, with 3½" (9 cm) added for ease.

Sweater shown measures 39½" (100.5 cm) and fits a 36" (91.5 cm) bust.

Yarn

Sport weight (#2 Fine).

Shown here: Quince & Co. Chickadee (100% wool; 181 yd [166 m]/1¾ [50 g]): #109 Peacock, 8 (9, 10, 11, 12, 14, 14, 15, 16, 17) hanks.

Needles

Size U.S. 6 (4 mm): 32" (80 cm) circular (cir) and set of 4 or 5 double-pointed (dpn).

Adjust needle size if necessary to obtain the correct gauge.

Notions

Markers (m); removable markers; cable needle (cn); stitch holders or waste yarn; yarn needle, one 1½" (3.8 cm) or 2" (5 cm) button.

Gauge

24 sts (1 stitch repeat) = 3½" (9 cm) and 34 rows = 4" (10 cm) in Cable Rib Pattern.

26 sts and 32 rnds = 4" (10 cm) in St st worked in rnds.

Notes

⁓ When the pattern calls for transferring stitches and moving on to another section, it's advisable to mark the chart with the last row worked so that you can stop at the same row in the case of working the Right Front and Left Front, and know where in the pattern to pick up again when the pieces are joined for the yoke.

⁓ Transfer markers in place.

⁓ All slipped stitches should be slipped pwise unless otherwise indicated.

⁓ Circular needle is recommended to accommodate large number of sts. Do not join; work back and forth in rows.

back

With cir needle, CO 116 (128, 136, 148, 156, 168, 176, 184, 196, 204) sts. Do not join; work back and forth in rows.

EST MEDALLION CABLE CHART

Row 1: (WS) K1, [k1, p1] 6 (3, 5, 2, 4, 1, 3, 5, 2, 4) time(s), k1, pm, work from Medallion Cable Chart over next 88 (112, 112, 136, 136, 160, 160, 160, 184, 184) sts, pm, k1, [p1, k1] 6 (3, 5, 2, 4, 1, 3, 5, 2, 4) time(s), k1.

Row 2: K1, [p1, k1] 6 (3, 5, 2, 4, 1, 3, 5, 2, 4) time(s), p1, slm, cont Medallion Cable Chart to m, slm, p1, [k1, p1] 6 (3, 5, 2, 4, 1, 3, 5, 2, 4) time(s), k1.

Cont working as est through Row 24 of Medallion Cable Chart, then work Rows 1–14 once more.

EST CABLE RIB CHART

Next Row: (WS) Cont in ribbing as est to m, slm, work from Cable Rib Chart to m, slm, cont in ribbing as est to end.

Cont as est, working ribbing and Cable Rib Chart until piece meas 10¾ (11, 11¼, 11½, 11½, 11½, 11½, 11½, 11½, 11½)" (27.5 [28, 28.5, 29, 29, 29, 29, 29, 29, 29] cm) from CO edge, ending after a WS row.

SHAPE ARMHOLES

Row 1: (RS) Work in ribbing as est to m, slm, k2tog, work in Cable Rib patt as est to 2 sts before m, ssk, slm, work in ribbing as est to m—2 sts dec'd.

Row 2: (WS) Work in ribbing as est to m, slm, p2tog tbl, work in Cable Rib patt as est to 2 sts before m, p2tog, slm, work in ribbing as est to m—2 sts dec'd.

Rep last 2 rows 2 more times—104 (116, 124, 136, 144, 156, 164, 172, 184, 192) sts rem.

Next Row: (RS) BO 10 (4, 8, 2, 6, 0, 4, 8, 2, 6) sts in patt, work in ribbing as est to m, slm, work in Cable Rib patt as est to m, slm, work in ribbing as est to end.

Next Row: BO 10 (4, 8, 2, 6, 0, 4, 8, 2, 6) sts in patt, work in ribbing as est to m, slm, work in Cable Rib patt as est to m, slm, k1, p1, k1—84 (108, 108, 132, 132, 156, 156, 156, 180, 180) sts.

Work even in patt as est, knitting first and last st of each row until armhole meas 7 (7¼, 7½, 7¾, 8, 8¼, 8½, 8½, 8¾, 9)" (18 [18.5, 19, 19.5, 20.5, 21, 21.5, 21.5, 22, 23] cm), ending after a WS row.

Place Back sts onto st holder or waste yarn. Break yarn.

MEDALLION CABLE CHART

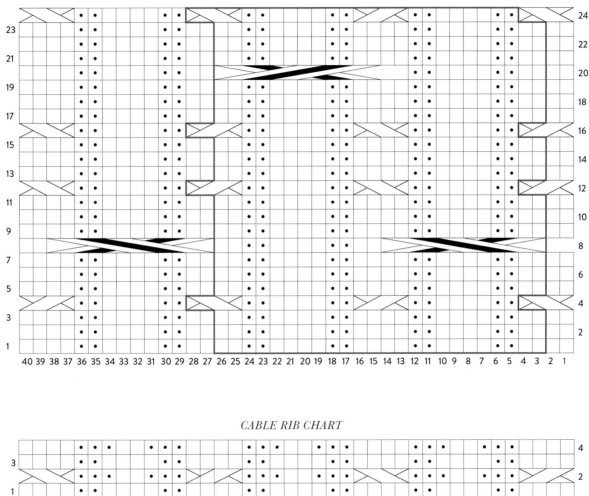

CABLE RIB CHART

	knit on RS, purl on WS		sl 6 sts to cn, hold to front, k2, p2, k2, [k2, p2, k2] from cn
•	purl on RS, knit on WS		
	sl 2 sts to cn, hold to front, k2, k2 from cn		sl 6 sts to cn, hold to back, k2, p2, k2, [k2, p2, k2] from cn
	sl 2 sts to cn, hold to back, k2, k2 from cn		repeat pattern

right front

With cir needle, CO 9 (12, 14, 17, 19, 22, 24, 26, 29, 31) sts, pm, CO 40 sts, pm, CO 9 (12, 14, 17, 19, 22, 24, 26, 29, 31) sts—58 (64, 68, 74, 78, 84, 88, 92, 98, 102) sts. Do not join; work back and forth in rows.

Set-up Row 1: (WS) Work Row 1 of Right Front Cable Chart in selected size to m, slm, work Row 1 of Medallion Cable Chart over next 40 sts, slm, work Row 1 of Right Front Cable Chart in selected size to end.

Set-up Row 2: (RS) K1, work even to 1 st before m, knitting the knit sts and purling the purl sts, k1, slm, work Row 2 of Medallion Cable Chart to m, slm, k1, work even to last st, knitting the knit sts and purling the purl sts, k1.

EST PATTS

Row 1: Work Row 1 of Right Front Cable Chart in selected size to m, slm, work next row of Medallion Cable Chart to m, slm, work Row 1 of Right Front Cable Chart in selected size to end.

Row 2: Work Row 2 of Right Front Cable Chart in selected size to m, slm, work next row of Medallion Cable Chart to m, slm, work Row 2 of Right Front Cable Chart in selected size to end.

Rep last 2 rows until piece meas 5¼ (5½, 5¾, 5¾, 5¾, 5¾, 5¾, 5¾, 5¾, 5¾)" (13.5 [14, 14.5, 14.5, 14.5, 14.5, 14.5, 14.5, 14.5, 14.5] cm) from CO edge, ending after a WS row.

BUTTON BAND

Row 1: (RS) Use the Knitted Cast-on method (see Glossary) to CO 18 sts. Do not turn. K1, [k1, p2] 5 times, k2, cont in patt as est to end—76 (82, 86, 92, 96, 102, 106, 110, 116, 120) sts.

Row 2: Work in patt as est to last 18 sts, k1, [p1, k2] 5 times, p1, k1.

Cont working in patts as est until button band meas ¾" (2 cm), ending after a WS row.

Buttonhole Row: (RS) Work in patt as est over first 6 sts, BO 6 sts in patt, work in patt as est to end.

Next Row: Work in patt as est to BO sts, use the Backward Loop method (see Glossary) to CO 6 sts, work in patt as est to end.

Cont working in patts as est until button band meas 1½" (3.8 cm), ending after a RS row.

BEGIN EXPANDED PLAIT CHART

Next Row: (WS) Work in patts as est to last 18 sts, k1, work 16 sts in Expanded Plait Chart, k1.

Cont working in patts as est until piece meas 10¾ (11, 11¼, 11½, 11½, 11½, 11½, 11½, 11½, 11½)" (27.5 [28, 28.5, 29, 29, 29, 29, 29, 29, 29] cm) from CO edge, ending after a RS row.

Mark the last st of the row with a removable m for seaming, then cont in patt as est until piece meas 7 (7¼, 7½, 7¾, 8, 8¼, 8½, 8½, 8¾, 9)" (18 [18.5, 19, 19.5, 20.5, 21, 21.5, 21.5, 22, 23] cm) from m, ending after a WS row.

Place Right Front sts onto st holder or waste yarn. Break yarn.

left front

Work same as Right Front, working Left Front Cable Chart in place of Right Front Cable Chart until piece meas 5¼ (5½, 5¾, 5¾, 5¾, 5¾, 5¾, 5¾, 5¾, 5¾)" (13.5 [14, 14.5, 14.5, 14.5, 14.5, 14.5, 14.5, 14.5, 14.5] cm) from CO edge, ending after a RS row.

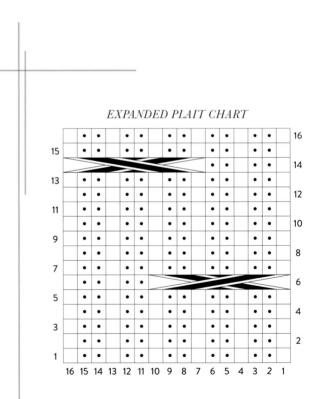

EXPANDED PLAIT CHART

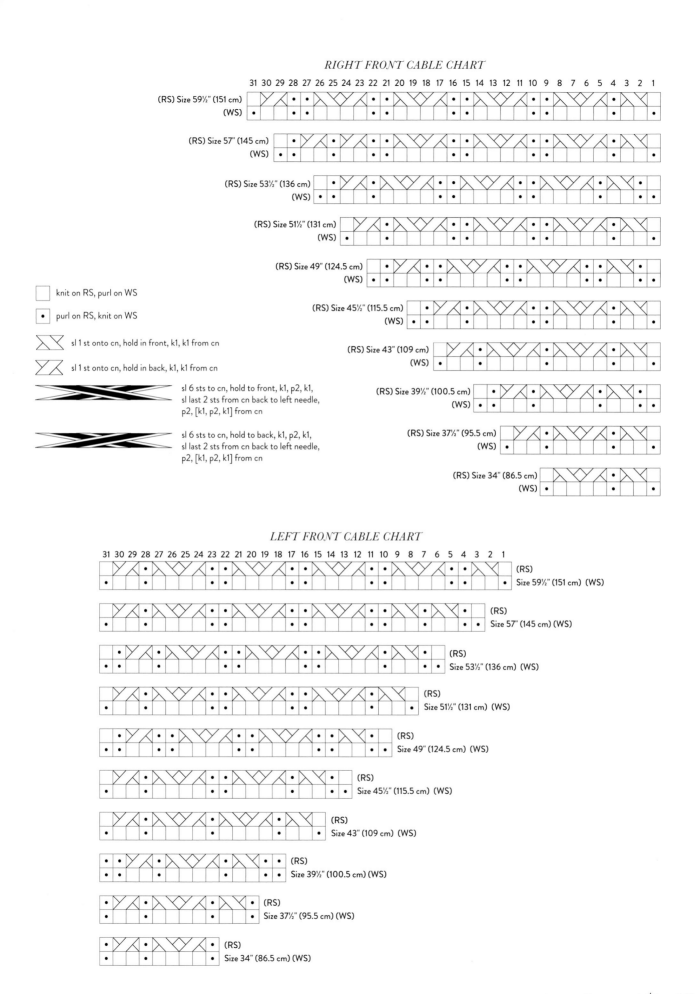

RIGHT FRONT CABLE CHART

knit on RS, purl on WS

purl on RS, knit on WS

sl 1 st onto cn, hold in front, k1, k1 from cn

sl 1 st onto cn, hold in back, k1, k1 from cn

sl 6 sts to cn, hold to front, k1, p2, k1,
sl last 2 sts from cn back to left needle,
p2, [k1, p2, k1] from cn

sl 6 sts to cn, hold to back, k1, p2, k1,
sl last 2 sts from cn back to left needle,
p2, [k1, p2, k1] from cn

LEFT FRONT CABLE CHART

BUTTON BAND

Row 1: (WS) Use the Knitted Cast-on method to CO 18 sts. Do not turn. K1, [p1, k2] 5 times, k1, p1, cont in patt as est to end—76 (82, 86, 92, 96, 102, 106, 110, 116, 120) sts.

Row 2: Work in patt as est to last 18 sts, k1, [k1, p2] 5 times, k2.

Rep last 2 rows until button band meas 1½" (3.8 cm), ending after a RS row.

EST EXPANDED PLAIT CHART

Next Row: (WS) K1, work 16 sts in Expanded Plait Chart, k1, cont in patt as est to end.

Cont working in patt as est until piece meas 10¾ (11, 11¼, 11½, 11½, 11½, 11½, 11½, 11½, 11½)" (27.5 [28, 28.5, 29, 29, 29, 29, 29, 29, 29] cm) from CO edge, ending after a RS row.

Mark the first st of the row with a removable m for seaming, then cont in patt as est until piece meas 7 (7¼, 7½, 7¾, 8, 8¼, 8½, 8½, 8¾, 9)" (18 [18.5, 19, 19.5, 20.5, 21, 21.5, 21.5, 22, 23] cm) from m, ending after a WS row.

Break yarn.

yoke

Return 84 (108, 108, 132, 132, 156, 156, 156, 180, 180) held Back and 76 (82, 86, 92, 96, 102, 106, 110, 116, 120) held Right Front sts to cir needle with the Left Front sts—236 (272, 280, 316, 324, 360, 368, 376, 412, 420) sts.

Rejoin yarn to Right Front with RS facing. Cont working back and forth in rows as foll:

Dec Row 1: (RS) Work in patt as est to end of Right Front, [k1, p1] 2 times to first m on Back, slm, k2tog, work in patt across Back as est to 2 sts before next m, ssk, slm, [p1, k1] 2 times, work in patt across Left Front as est to end—2 Back sts dec'd.

Dec Row 2: Work in patt as est to third m (first m on Back), slm, p2tog tbl, work in patt as est to 2 sts before next m, p2tog, slm, work in patt as est to end—2 Back sts dec'd.

Rep last 2 rows 1 (6, 4, 10, 9, 13, 12, 10, 15, 15) more time(s)—76 (80, 88, 88, 92, 100, 104, 108, 116, 116) sts rem for Back; 228 (244, 260, 272, 284, 304, 316, 328, 348, 356) total sts rem.

Sizes 34 (37½, 43, 45½, 51½, 59½)"
(86.5 [95.5, 109, 115.5, 131, 151] cm) Only
Next Row: (RS) Work even in patts as est.

Sizes 39½ (49, 53½, 57)" (100.5 [124.5, 136, 145] cm) Only
Rep Dec Row 1 once more—86 (98, 106, 114) sts rem across back; 258 (302, 326, 346) total sts.

All Sizes
Next Row: (WS) Work in patt as est to end without dec further.

SHAPE RIGHT COLLAR
Work in Welt Patt

Row 1: (RS) Work in patt as est to m, slm, knit to m, slm, work in patt as est over next 8 (11, 13, 16, 18, 21, 23, 25, 28, 30) sts, place a contrasting marker for collar, sl1, k1, psso, turn—1 Back st dec'd.

Row 2: (WS) Sl1, slm, work in patt as est to m, knit to m, slm, work in patt as est to end.

Row 3: Work in patt as est to m, slm, purl to m, slm, work in patt as est to collar m, slm, sl1, k1, psso, turn—1 Back st dec'd.

Row 4: Rep Row 2.

Row 5: Rep Row 1—1 Back st dec'd.

Begin Rib Cable Chart

Row 1: Sl1, work in patt as est to end.

Row 2: Work in patt as est to m, slm, work in Rib Cable Chart to m, slm, work in patt as est to collar m, slm, sl1, k1, psso, turn—1 Back st dec'd.

Rep last 2 rows 24 (26, 30, 30, 32, 35, 38, 39, 43, 44) more times— 200 (214, 225, 238, 248, 263, 274, 283, 299, 308) sts rem.

Work in Welt Patt

Set-up Row: (RS) [Knit to m, remove m] 2 times, knit to next m, slm, sl1, k1, psso, turn—1 Back st dec'd.

Row 1: (WS) Sl1, slm, knit to end.

Row 2: K1, purl to m, slm, sl1, k1, psso, turn—1 Back st dec'd.

Row 3: Rep Row 1.

Row 4: Knit to m, slm, sl1, k1, psso, turn—1 Back st dec'd.

Row 5: Sl1, slm, purl to last st, k1.

Row 6: Rep Row 4—1 Back st dec'd.

Rep last 6 rows 2 more times—190 (204, 215, 228, 238, 253, 264, 273, 289, 298) total sts.

Do not turn after last row. Keep yarn attached.

SHAPE LEFT COLLAR
Work in Welt Patt
Next Row: (RS) Knit to first m, slm, work in patt as est to 2 sts before next m, ssk, slm, knit to m, slm, work in patt as est to end—189 (203, 214, 227, 237, 252, 263, 272, 288, 297) sts rem.

Row 1: (WS) Work in patt as est to m, slm, knit to m, slm, work in patt as est over next 8 (11, 13, 16, 18, 21, 23, 25, 28, 30) sts, place a contrasting m for collar, sl1, p1, psso, turn—1 Back st dec'd.

Row 2: (RS) Sl1, slm, work in patt as est to m, slm, purl to m, slm, work in patt as est to end.

Row 3: Work in patt as est to m, slm, knit to m, sl m, work in patt as est to next m, slm, sl1, p1, psso, turn—1 Back st dec'd.

Row 4: Sl1, slm, work in patt as est to m, slm, knit to m, slm, work in patt as est to end.

Begin Rib Cable Chart
Row 1: (WS) Work in patt as est to m, work from Rib Cable Chart to m, slm, work in patt as est to collar m, slm, sl1, p1, psso, turn—1 Back st dec'd.

Row 2: Sl1, slm, work in patt as est to end.

Rep last 2 rows 24 (26, 30, 30, 32, 35, 38, 39, 43, 44) more times, then rep Row 1 once more—162 (174, 182, 194, 202, 214, 222, 230, 242, 250) sts rem.

Work in Welt Patt
Row 1: (RS) Sl1, slm, knit to end.

Row 2: Knit to collar m, slm, sl1, p1, psso, turn—1 Back st dec'd.

Row 3: Sl1, purl to last st, k1.

Row 4: Rep Row 2—1 Back st dec'd.

Row 5: Rep Row 1.

Row 6: K1, purl to collar m, slm, sl1, p1, psso, turn—1 Back st dec'd.

Rep last 6 rows 2 times, then rep Rows 1 and 2 once more—152 (164, 172, 184, 192, 204, 212, 220, 232, 240) sts rem. Do not break yarn.

Divide 76 (82, 86, 92, 96, 102, 106, 110, 116, 120) Right and Left Collar sts onto separate needles, hold parallel with WS together and graft together using 3-Needle Bind-off method (see Glossary).

Seam the body, beg 2" (5 cm) from hem to the underarm, using whip stitch for a pronounced seam or mattress stitch for an invisible seam.

sleeves

With cir needle and RS facing, beg at underarm seam, pick up and knit 64 (66, 70, 78, 80, 90, 100, 106, 110, 114) evenly around armhole. Do not join; work back and forth in rows.

Est St st, knitting the first and last st of each row for selvedge.

Work 21 (21, 15, 9, 9, 5, 3, 3, 3, 3) rows even.

Dec Row: (RS) K1, k2tog, knit to last 3 sts, ssk, k1—2 sts dec'd.

Rep last 22 (22, 16, 10, 10, 6, 4, 4, 4, 4) rows 4 (4, 6, 9, 10, 14, 19, 21, 23, 24) more times—54 (56, 56, 58, 58, 60, 60, 62, 62, 64) sts.

Cont in St st as est until sleeve meas 14¼ (14½, 14½, 14¾, 14¾, 14¾, 14¾, 14¾, 14¾, 14¾)" (36 [37, 37, 37.5, 37.5, 37.5, 37.5, 37.5, 37.5, 37.5] cm) from underarm, ending after a WS row.

CUFF

Rows 1, 3, 4, and 6: Knit.

Rows 2 and 5: K1, purl to last st, k1.

Next Row: (WS) BO all sts purlwise.

finishing

Starting at the cuff, seam sleeves closed.

Weave in ends. Block to measurements.

Sew button onto the RS of bottom of Left Front button band, lining it up with the buttonhole on the opposite band.

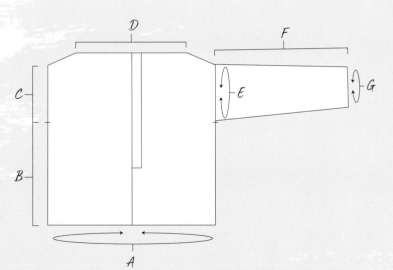

A: 34 (37½, 39½, 43, 45½, 49, 51½, 53½, 57, 59½)"
86.5 [95.5, 100.5, 109, 115.5, 124.5, 131, 136, 145, 151] cm)

B: 10¾ (11, 11¼, 11½, 11½, 11½, 11½, 11½, 11½, 11½)"
27.5 [28, 28.5, 29, 29, 29, 29, 29, 29, 29] cm)

C: 7 (7¼, 7½, 7¾, 8, 8¼, 8½, 8½, 8¾, 9)"
18 [18.5, 19, 19.5, 20.5, 21, 21.5, 21.5, 22, 23] cm)

D: 11 (11¾, 12¾, 12¾, 13½, 14½, 15¼, 15¾, 17, 17)"
28 [30, 32.5, 32.5, 34.5, 37, 38.5, 40, 43, 43] cm)

E: 9¾ (10¼, 10¾, 12, 12¼, 13¾, 15½, 16¼, 17, 17½)"
25 [26, 27.5, 30.5, 31, 35, 39.5, 41.5, 43, 44.5] cm)

F: 15 (15¼, 15¼, 15½, 15½, 15½, 15½, 15½, 15½, 15½)"
38 [38.5, 38.5, 39.5, 39.5, 39.5, 39.5, 39.5, 39.5, 39.5] cm)

G: 8 (8¼, 8¼, 8½, 8½, 8¾, 8¾, 9, 9, 9¼)"
20.5 [21, 21, 21.5, 21.5, 22, 22, 23, 23, 23.5] cm)

demetria
raglan

Greek; goddess of harvest

From the delicate pin-striping to the raglan yoke, Demetria is not only as soft as
a cloud, but also thin, lightweight, and extremely cozy due to the nature of the
colorwork and casual fit. Rather than using color stranding to produce the vertical
stripes, you'll work them in a mosaic-style slip stitch so that only one color is used
for each round. This is a great alternative to color stranding, especially for folks
not familiar or comfortable with two-color knitting.

Finished Sizes
36 (37¼, 38¾, 41¼, 43½,
45¼, 47½, 49¾, 51½)" (91.5
[94.5, 98.5, 105, 110.5, 115,
120.5, 126.5, 131] cm) bust
circumference.

Designed to fit 33 (34¼,
35¾, 38¼, 40½, 42¼,
44½, 46¾, 48½)" (84 [87,
91, 97, 103, 107.5, 113,
118.5, 123] cm) bust, with
3" (7.5 cm) added for ease.

Sweater shown measures
38¾" (98.5 cm) and fits a
35¾" (91 cm) bust.

Yarn
Sport weight (#2 Fine).

Shown here: Woolfolk Sno
(100% Ovis 21 Ultimate
Merino wool; 223 yd

[204 m]/1¾ [50 g]): #01+11
(A), 3 (3, 3, 3, 4, 4, 4, 5, 5)
hanks; #02+09 (B), 3 (3, 3,
3, 4, 4, 4, 5, 5) hanks.

> **Note:** *For a longer sweater,
> purchase 1 more hank of
> each color for every addi-
> tional 6" (15 cm) of desired
> length.*

Needles
Yoke, body, and sleeves:
Size U.S. 5 (3.75 mm):
16" (40 cm) and 32" (80 cm)
circular (cir) and set of 4 or 5
double-pointed (dpn).

Cuffs and hems: Size U.S. 4
(3.5 mm): 32" (80 cm) cir
and set of 4 or 5 dpn.

*Adjust needle size if necessary
to obtain the correct gauge.*

Notions
Markers (m), stitch holders
or waste yarn, yarn needle.

Gauge
28 sts and 28 rnds =
4" (10 cm) in Slip St Stripe,
worked in rnds on larger
needles, blocked.

> **Note:** *Because every other
> row is slipped, 56 rnds
> worked looks like 28 rnds.*

Notes
— Cowlneck is worked from
the top down in rnds.

— When working Slip St
Stripe, allow long floats across
the back of the slipped stitch
so that the fabric maintains
stretch.

SLIP ST STRIPE (MULTIPLE OF 2 STS)
Rnd 1: *Using color B, sl1 pwise wyb, k1; rep from * to end.

Rnd 2: *Using color A, k1, sl1 pwise wyb; rep from * to end.

Rep Rnds 1 and 2 for patt.

neck

Using color A and smaller dpns, CO 100 (104, 108, 116, 120, 128, 132, 136, 144) sts. Pm for beg of rnd and join for working in rnds, being careful not to twist sts.

Next Rnd: *K1, p1; rep from * to end.

Rep last rnd 3 more times.

Knit 1 rnd.

Change to larger dpns or 16" (40 cm) cir needles. Join color B and work Slip St Stripe patt (see Stitch Guide) until piece meas 3" (7.5 cm) from CO edge.

yoke

Set-up Rnd: Work in Slip St Stripe patt for 20 (21, 22, 24, 25, 27, 27, 29, 30) sts, work 1 st and mark for raglan, work 7 (7, 7, 7, 7, 7, 9, 7, 9) sts for left sleeve, work 1 st and mark for raglan, work 41 (43, 45, 49, 51, 55, 55, 59, 61) sts across front, work 1 st and mark for raglan, work 7 (7, 7, 7, 7, 7, 9, 7, 9) sts for right sleeve, work 1 st and mark for raglan, work 21 (22, 23, 25, 26, 28, 28, 30, 31) sts, ending at center back.

SHAPE RAGLAN

Note: Change to longer cir needle when necessary.

Next Rnd: Work in Slip St Stripe patt as est to end.

Inc Rnd: *Work in Slip St Stripe patt as est to marked st, [k1, yo, k1] into st; rep from * 3 more times, work to end—8 sts inc'd.

Next Rnd: Work in Slip St Stripe patt as est to end.

Rep last 3 rnds 34 (35, 37, 39, 42, 43, 47, 49, 51) more times—380 (392, 412, 436, 464, 480, 516, 536, 560) sts; 111 (115, 121, 129, 137, 143, 151, 159, 165) sts each Back and Front and 77 (79, 83, 87, 93, 95, 105, 107, 113) sts each Sleeve.

DIVIDE BODY AND SLEEVES
Next Rnd: Work in Slip St Stripe patt as est to first marked st, *use the Backward Loop method (see Glossary) to CO 15 sts, transfer 79 (81, 85, 89, 95, 97, 107, 109, 115) sts onto st holder or waste yarn for Sleeve, work to next marked st; rep from * once more, work as est to end—252 (260, 272, 288, 304, 316, 332, 348, 360) sts rem.

body

Work even in Slip St Stripe patt as est until piece meas 11 (11¼, 11½, 12, 12¼, 12½, 12¾, 13½, 13½)" (28 [28.5, 29, 30.5, 31, 32, 32.5, 34.5, 34.5] cm) from divide, or to desired length.

Note: This is a slightly cropped sweater, and you may want to make it longer at this point to suit your personal style.

Break color A.

Change to smaller cir needle.

Using color B, knit 1 rnd.

EST 1×1 RIBBING
Next Rnd: *P1, k1; rep from * to end.

Rep last rnd 3 more times.

BO all sts loosely in patt.

sleeves

Using the opposite color as used on the last rnd of Yoke, and larger dpns, beg at the st left of the center of the underarm CO sts, pick up and knit 7 sts, transfer 79 (81, 85, 89, 95, 97, 107, 109, 115) Sleeve sts to needle and cont in Slip St Stripe patt as est to end, pick up and knit 8 sts from rem underarm CO sts—94 (96, 100, 104, 110, 112, 124, 130, 134) sts. Pm for beg of rnd and join for working in rnds.

SHAPE SLEEVE

Work even in Slip St Stripe patt as est for 9 (9, 9, 9, 7, 7, 5, 4, 4) rnds.

Dec Rnd: Work even in patt to last 2 sts, sl2, remove m, k1, p2sso, pm—2 sts dec'd.

Rep last 10 (10, 10, 10, 8, 8, 6, 5, 5) rnds 17 (17, 18, 19, 22, 23, 27, 28, 30) more times—58 (60, 62, 64, 64, 64, 66, 66, 68) sts.

Cont working even in Slip St Stripe patt as est until piece meas 15 (15½, 15½, 15½, 16, 16, 16, 16, 16)" (38 [39.5, 39.5, 39.5, 40.5, 40.5, 40.5, 40.5, 40.5] cm) from underarm.

Break color A.

Change to smaller dpns.

Using color B, knit 1 rnd.

EST 1×1 RIBBING

Next Rnd: *P1, k1; rep from * to end.

Rep last rnd 3 more times.

BO all sts loosely in patt.

finishing

Weave in ends and block to measurements.

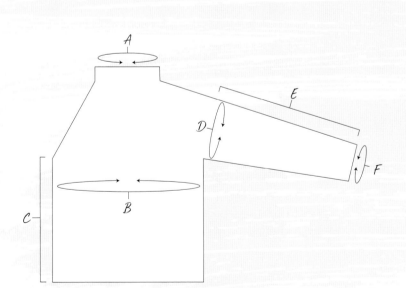

A: 14¼ (14¾, 15½, 16½, 17¼, 18¼, 18¾, 19½, 20½)" 36 [37.5, 39.5, 42, 44, 46.5, 47.5, 49.5, 52] cm

B: 36 (37¼, 38¾, 41¼, 43½, 45¼, 47½, 49¾, 51½)" 91.5 [94.5, 98.5, 105, 110.5, 115, 120.5, 126.5, 131] cm)

C: 11¼ (11½, 11¾, 12¼, 12½, 12¾, 13, 13¾, 13¾)" 28.5 [29, 30, 31, 32, 32.5, 33, 35, 35] cm)

D: 13½ (13¾, 14¼, 14¾, 15¾, 16, 17½, 17¾, 18½)" 34.5 [35, 36, 37.5, 40, 40.5, 44.5, 45, 47] cm)

E: 15 (15½, 15½, 15½, 16, 16, 16, 16, 16)" 38 [39.5, 39.5, 39.5, 40.5, 40.5, 40.5, 40.5, 40.5] cm)

F: 8¼ (8½, 8¾, 9¼, 9¼, 9¼, 9½, 9½, 9¾)" 21 [21.5, 22, 23.5, 23.5, 23.5, 24, 24, 25] cm)

Glossary

CAST-ONS

Backward Loop Cast-on

*Loop working yarn as shown and place it on the needle backward with right leg of loop in back of the needle. Repeat from *.

Channel Island Cast-on

Measure out tail, about 1" (2.5 cm) per stitch cast on, and fold in half. Near the tail of the folded length, create a slipknot with the doubled yarn and place it on the right needle (this does not count as a stitch) (*fig. 1*). Holding the short tail out of the way, *wrap the double strand tail around the left thumb counterclockwise twice, bring working yarn over the needle, creating a yo (*fig. 2*), then insert the needle under the two wraps around the thumb, catch the working yarn as you would with a standard long-tail cast on, bring the yarn through the two wraps (*fig. 3*), releasing them from the thumb, and pull snug against the needle; rep from * until reaching the desired number of stitches.

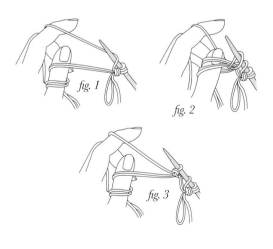

fig. 1

fig. 2

fig. 3

Knitted Cast-on

If there are no stitches on the needles, make a slipknot of working yarn and place it on the left needle. When there is at least one stitch on the left needle, *use the right needle to knit the first stitch (or slipknot) on the left needle (*fig. 1*) and place the new loop onto the left needle to form a new stitch (*fig. 2*). Repeat from * for the desired number of stitches, always working into the last stitch made.

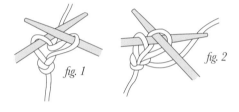

fig. 1

fig. 2

Crochet Provisional Cast-on

This cast-on method is worked with a crochet hook. Use waste yarn for the chain and then knit a plain row with the working yarn (the provisional cast-on is not complete until there is a row of working yarn stitches on the needle).

Place a slipknot on a crochet hook. Hold the knitting needle and yarn in your left hand and hook in your right hand, with yarn under the needle. Place the hook over the needle, wrap yarn around the hook, and pull the loop through the loop on the hook (*fig. 1*). *Bring yarn to back under the needle, wrap yarn around the hook, and pull it through the loop on the hook (*fig. 2*). Repeat from * until there is one fewer stitch than the desired number on the needle. Slip loop from hook to needle for the last stitch.

fig. 1

fig. 2

BIND-OFFS

3-needle Bind-off

Place stitches to be joined onto two separate needles. Hold them with right sides of knitting facing together (unless otherwise specified). Insert a third needle into first stitch on each of the other two needles (*fig. 1*) and knit them together as one stitch (*fig. 2*). *Knit next stitch on each needle the same way. Pass first stitch over second stitch (*fig. 3*). Repeat from * until one stitch remains on third needle. Cut yarn and pull tail through last stitch.

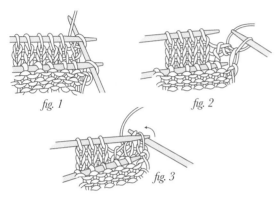

fig. 1

fig. 2

fig. 3

Elastic Bind-off

K2. *Insert LH needle into the front of the 2 sts on the RH needle (*fig. 1*). Knit the sts together tbl, k1 (*fig. 2*). Rep from * to end.

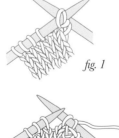

fig. 1

fig. 2

1×1 Elastic Bind-off

K2. Insert LH needle into the front of the 2 sts on the RH needle. Knit the sts together tbl, *p1, purl 2 sts on RH needle together, k1, knit 2 sts on RH needle together tbl; rep from * to last st, k1, knit to sts on RH needle together tbl.

ABBREVIATIONS

beg begin(ning)

BO bind off

brk Knit stitch with paired yarn over together

brp Purl stitch with paired yarn over together

CC contrasting color

cir circular needle

cn cable needle

CO cast on

cont continue

dec/dec'd decrease/ decreased

dpn(s) double-pointed needle(s)

est established

foll follows

g grams

inc/inc'd increase/ increased

k knit

kfb knit into the front and back

kwise knitwise

k2tog knit 2 together

k3tog knit 3 together

LH left-hand

m marker

MC main color

M1 and M1L Make 1 left

M1R Make 1 right

meas measure(s)

p purl

patt pattern

pm place marker

psso pass slip stitch over

pwise purlwise

rem remain(ing)

rep repeat

RH right-hand

rnd(s) round(s)

RS right side

sl slip

slm slip marker

sl1 Slip 1 st pwise unless specified; when slipping st with RS facing, hold working yarn to the back, with WS facing, hold working yarn to the front; when slipping st for selvedge, slip st pwise, then bring working yarn to the back between slipped st and next st on LH needle.

sl1yo Slip next stitch on the needle pwise with yarn in front

sl2, k1, p2sso Slip 2 sts together knitwise (as if to k2tog), k1, pass the 2 slipped sts over the knit st.

ssk slip, slip, knit

sssk slip, slip, slip, knit

st(s) stitch(es)

St st stockinette stitch

tbl through back loop

WS wrong side

yo yarnover

wyb with yarn in back

wyf with yarn in front

* repeat starting point

[ ] work instructions as a group a specified number of times, or metric equivalents

I-cord Bind-off

With live sts on left needle and right side facing, *k1, knit 2 together through the back loops (*fig. 1*), and transfer the two stitches from the right needle to the left needle (*fig. 2*). Repeat from * until all stitches have been bound off.

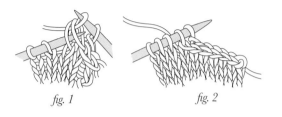

fig. 1   *fig. 2*

Sewn Bind-off

Cut the yarn three times the width of the knitting to be bound off, and thread it onto a yarn needle. Working from left to right, *insert the yarn needle through the first two stitches (*fig. 1*), pull the yarn through, then bring the needle back through the first stitch (*fig. 2*), pull the yarn through, and slip this stitch off the knitting needle. Repeat from *.

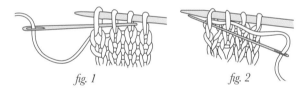

fig. 1   *fig. 2*

INCREASE STITCHES

Knit 1 into Front & Back (kfb)

Knit into a stitch but leave it on the left needle (*fig. 1*), then knit through the back loop of the same stitch (*fig. 2*) and slip the original stitch off the needle (*fig. 3*).

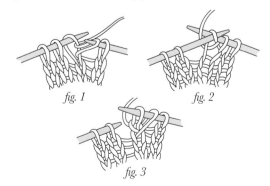

fig. 1   *fig. 2*

fig. 3

Left Slant (M1L) & Standard M1

> *Note: Use the left slant if no direction of slant is specified.*

With the left needle tip, lift the strand between the last knitted stitch and the first stitch on the left needle from front to back (*fig. 1*), then knit the lifted loop through the back (*fig. 2*).

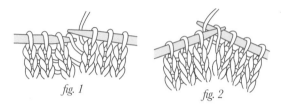

fig. 1   *fig. 2*

Right Slant (M1R)

With the left needle tip, lift the strand between the needles from back to front (*fig. 1*). Knit the lifted loop through the front (*fig. 2*).

For the purl versions (M1P, M1LP, and M1RP), work as above, purling the lifted loop.

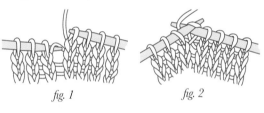

fig. 1   *fig. 2*

DECREASE STITCHES

sl2, k1, p2sso

Slip 2 sts together knitwise (as if to k2tog), k1, pass the 2 slipped sts over the knit st.

Slip, Slip, Knit (ssk)

Slip two stitches individually knitwise (*fig. 1*), insert the left needle tip into the front of these two slipped stitches, and use the right needle to knit them together through the back loops (*fig. 2*).

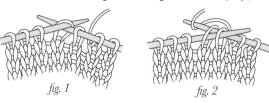

fig. 1   *fig. 2*

DECREASE CONTINUED

Slip, Slip, Slip, Knit [sssk]

Slip three sts individually knitwise (*fig. 1*), insert the left needle tip into the front of these three slipped sts, and use the right needle to knit them together through the back loops (*fig. 2*).

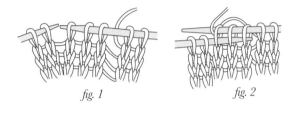

fig. 1   *fig. 2*

SHORT-ROWS

Close Gaps

RS: Work to 1 stitch before gap, *lift the slipped stitch below next the stitch onto left-hand needle (*fig. 1*) and knit it together with the last stitch before gap; repeat from * as indicated in pattern.

WS: Work to 1 stitch before gap, *lift the slipped stitch below next stitch onto left-hand needle (*fig. 2*) and purl it together tbl with the last stitch before gap; repeat from * as indicated in pattern.

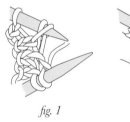 

fig. 1   *fig. 2*

SEAMING

Mattress Stitch

With RS of knitting facing, use threaded needle to pick up one bar between first two stitches on one piece, then corresponding bar plus the bar above it on other piece. *Pick up next two bars on first piece, then next two bars on other (*fig. 1*). Repeat from * to end of seam, finishing by picking up last bar (or pair of bars) at the top of first piece.

fig. 1

Kitchener Stitch

1. Bring threaded needle through front stitch as if to purl and leave stitch on needle (*fig. 1*).

2. Bring threaded needle through back stitch as if to knit and leave stitch on needle (*fig. 2*).

3. Bring threaded needle through first front stitch as if to knit and slip this stitch off needle. Bring threaded needle through next front stitch as if to purl and leave stitch on needle (*fig. 3*).

4. Bring threaded needle through first back stitch as if to purl and slip this stitch off needle. Bring needle through next back stitch as if to knit and leave stitch on needle (*fig. 4*).

5. Repeat Steps 3 and 4 until no stitches remain on needles.

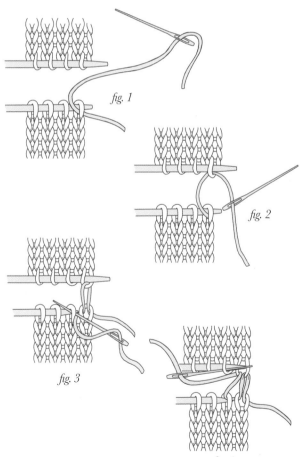

fig. 1

fig. 2

fig. 3

fig. 4

DUPLICATE STITCH

Horizontal: Bring threaded needle out from back to front at the base of the V of the knitted stitch you want to cover. *Working right to left, pass needle in and out under the stitch in the row above it and back into the base of the same stitch. Bring needle back out at the base of the V of the next stitch to the left. Repeat from * *(fig. 1)*.

Vertical: Beginning at lowest point, work as for horizontal duplicate stitch, ending by bringing the needle back out at the base of the stitch directly above the stitch just worked *(fig.2)*.

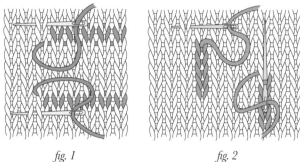

fig. 1   *fig. 2*

COMMON STITCHES

Garter Stitch
When working in the rnd:
Rnd 1: Knit

Rnd 2: Purl.

Rep rnds 1 and 2 for pattern.

When working flat:
Knit all sts, every row.

Stockinette Stitch
When working in rounds:
Knit all sts, every rnd.

When working in rows:
Knit on RS rows, purl on WS rows.

YARN SOURCES

Amano Yarns
amanoyarns.com

Berroco, Inc.
www.berroco.com

Blue Sky Fibers
blueskyfibers.com

Elsawool
www.wool-clothing.com

Hazel Knits
www.hazelknits.com

Hedgehog Fibres
shop.hedgehogfibres.com

Magpie Fibers
www.magpiefibers.com

Manos del Uruguay
Distributed in the U.S. by Fairmount Fibers
fairmountfibers.com

O-Wool
o-wool.com

Purl Soho
www.purlsoho.com

Quince & Co.
quinceandco.com

Shibui
shibuiknits.com

Stone Wool
thestonewool.co

Universal Yarn
universalyarn.com

Woolen Boon
woolenboon.com

Woolfolk
woolfolkyarn.com

YOTH Yarns
yothyarns.com

Acknowledgments

It's easy to forget how many people, how many voices, and how many hands work together to create a publication, especially a knitting book. The yarn support, editing, styling, and design that happen beyond the author are a choreographed effort that I wouldn't dream of doing alone.

I want to thank the team at Interweave and all the editors who worked so hard to make my vision come alive, especially Kerry Bogert, who has been with me from the seed of my first book, cheering me on through it all.

If you were reading through the very wordy parts thinking that I really know my stuff (and sound particularly clever), that's entirely thanks to Nathalie Mornu. She pushed me to dig deeper and get to the root of exactly what I wanted to convey with this book. Nathalie also provided the opportunity to make this project very personal, suggesting we share snippets of my process, over the years it took to get here, in Chapter One. Working with her was a true partnership.

My absolute gratitude goes to Kristen TenDyke for doing all of the dizzying tech editing—a job I couldn't fathom undertaking.

Partnerships with companies make it possible for me to design and produce. I want to thank each of the yarn companies that so generously supported this project. Please take a moment to check them out. Some of the patterns in this book feature yarn company spotlights. The people behind these companies took the time to provide some insight so that we can all peek a bit more deeply into their worlds.

Most of all, though, my husband provides the ultimate support. I went into this project knowing that I'd be knitting mostly large pieces and using a fair amount of fine yarns, yet I decided to knit all the samples myself rather than using sample knitters. Without someone there to nudge me along, encouraging and lifting me up, and showing unrivaled patience, I would have crumbled many times. So, thanks, Nate—you're my favorite.

Photo: Mare Pasley

ABOUT THE AUTHOR

Courtney Spainhower began working in fine art as a ceramicist. However, as a stay-at-home mother, she discovered knitting—the perfect blend of child-friendly and portable while fulfilling her need to keep her fidgeting hands busy and creating utilitarian pieces. She began designing as Pink Brutus Knits full-time in 2009. Since then, Courtney has contributed work to many books, yarn company collections, and magazines, including Interweave Knits, Knitscene, Berroco, Inc., Taproot, *and* Pom Pom Quarterly. *She released her first book,* Family-Friendly Knits, *in 2015.*

KNIT WITH INTENTION AND EXPAND YOUR KNITTING KNOW-HOW WITH THESE GREAT BOOKS FROM INTERWEAVE!

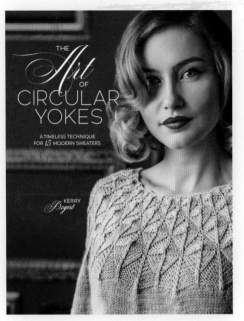

THE ART OF CIRCULAR YOKES

A Timeless Technique for 15 Modern Sweaters, by Kerry Bogert

9781632506719 | $26.99

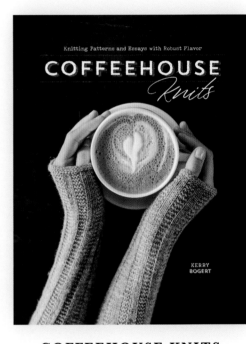

COFFEEHOUSE KNITS

Knitting Patterns and Essays with Robust Flavor, by Kerry Bogert

9781632506597 | $26.99

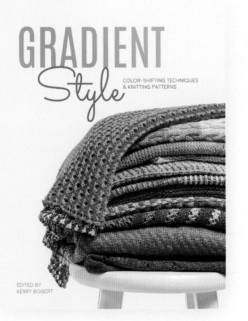

GRADIENT STYLE

Color-Shifting Techniques & Knitting Patterns, by Kerry Bogert

9781632506504 | $26.99